FARM-FRESH RECIPES

from the **Missing Goat Farm**

FARM-FRESH RECIPES

from the Missing Goat Farm

OVER 100 RECIPES INCLUDING PIES, SNACKS, SOUPS, BREADS, AND PRESERVES

HEATHER CAMERON

CICO BOOKS
LONDON NEW YORK

To my mom who is always there for me.
To my husband who supports me endlessly
and catches me when I fall.
And to Lily. My darling.
At the age of 4, you have taught me more
about life than I will ever be able to teach you.

Published in 2013 by CICO Books
An imprint of Ryland Peters & Small Ltd
20-21 Jockey's Fields, London, WC1R 4BW
519 Broadway, 5th Floor, New York, NY
10012

www.cicobooks.com

10 9 8 7 6 5 4 3 2 1

Text © Heather Cameron 2013
Design © CICO Books 2013

A CIP catalog record for this book is available from the Library of
Congress and the British Library.

ISBN 978 1 908862 60 0

Printed in China

Copy editor: Sarah Hoggett
Proofreader: Becky Alexander
Designer: ForgeForge Design
Stylist: Heather Cameron
Photographers: Heather Cameron, Kim Christie, and Janis Nicolay

RPS CICO BOOKS

For digital editions visit
www.cicobooks.com/apps.php

CONTENTS

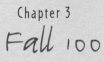

We grow the most amazing organic garlic every year. We lost track of the varieties, but it doesn't really matter—we know they are big, beautiful and delicious!

DID YOU CALL ME A FARMER?
I always dreamed of owning a farm ...

Since my early twenties, being a farmer and growing my own food seemed like a fabulous idea. This dream farm was always organic, had fancy feathered fowl, a few sheep, and a cow. I would preserve peaches, make jam, and bake pies for my loving family. How happy we would be.

On my 30th birthday, my husband, my mother, and I bought a farm together. It wasn't on purpose. It just came with the house we liked.

It was a small neglected blueberry farm 40 minutes outside of Vancouver, British Columbia. The day we moved, I cried for the entire 40-minute drive. I was leaving the city I loved and I was going to live with my mother. What was I thinking?

I had clearly gone mad. My experience with gardening consisted of watching Elliot Coleman, Martha Stewart, and "Little House on the Prairie" each week on television! I didn't even bring the one plant I owned from the city. I left it behind on the deck. What ... it was heavy!

The first few years, we bumbled our way through everything. Killing lavender plants by the dozens. Pruning apple trees to death. Drowning rhubarb plants and feeding my ridiculously expensive organic vegetable seeds to all the birds in the neighborhood. Darned if I knew why nothing was coming up.

To top it off, the house we bought ... well, it was ugly. Full of lace, paisley wallpaper, and blue office carpet. Our bathroom was dusty rose pink from left to right. This ugliness forced me to stay outside longer and educate myself.

PERHAPS, I COULD BE A FARMER ...

We learnt about zones, organic farming practices, and how to prune trees and shrubs properly.

The farm (yet to be named) was beautiful. Food and flowers grew in every corner. We were all very proud. I canned peaches and tomatoes. I made jam and apple sauce, and pickled beets. I also gutted the house and made it a home. We built a charming little shop called the Shabby Shack where I sold my own line of jams and jellies to the customers who came to buy blueberries. As the farm transformed, the number of customers increased. Our motto soon became, "Don't tell your friends!" This was working. I was happy. Maybe I am a farmer ...

WHY BE A FARMER, WHEN YOU CAN BE A STYLIST ...

I invited a magazine up from New York—*Victoria Magazine*. I offered them tea and homemade pie. They accepted. I never imagined they would. After the shock wore off, I put a priority list in place:
1. Learn to make pie.
2. Make everything look pretty.
3. Learn to make better pie.

The team spent two days at our farm. They were lovely and in the end, suggested I become a stylist for magazines. Not knowing what a stylist was, or that being a stylist was a real job, I laughed it off. Then, I stopped laughing and did some research. It was a job. Making things look pretty was a career! I was hooked and jumped in.

I spent ten years working for some of the top home decor and gardening magazines in North America. It was a dream job. I produced stories and styled homes, traveled to Paris, met fabulous people, and learnt how to take amazing photos. I turned my life into stories—magazine stories. How to make a greenhouse, how to re-design a guest bathroom. How to entertain in the shade. Decorating with shades of melon!

Life couldn't have been any better. Or so I thought.

We have about 10 raised beds for vegetables and strawberries. I prefer raised beds because I don't have to bend down so low and it helps stop the weeds from creeping in the sides.

WHY BE A STYLIST, WHEN YOU CAN BE A MOM ...

In 2007, I had a baby girl. My sweet Lily.

I made her organic apple sauce and purées. I started looking closer at food labels and hated what I read. There were so many preservatives and fillers. I taught myself to make bread, tortillas, and crackers for snacking, learnt to roast a whole chicken (after being a vegetarian for 20 years,) and made soup from scratch. Changed my jam recipes to slow-cook old-fashioned methods without the commercial pectin. We used these jams in yogurts, oatmeal, crêpes, and on cheese. Everything tasted better and I felt good about the food we were eating.

As Lily got older, she always joined me in the kitchen and garden. By older, I mean two. Her favorite thing to do was add a pinch of cinnamon to almost everything. I found I cared less about design and more about which snap pea variety to plant. Which sugar pumpkin would be good to roast in the fall.

Lily was eager to help in the garden too. I loved watching the joy on her face digging up potatoes and carrots. By three she knew almost all her vegetables and most of the herbs. My heart was happy.

In fall 2010, we placed an order for five baby chicks. By spring 2011, they were living in our house under the dining room table. Lily helped her dad build a chicken coop and by summer, we were collecting fresh eggs. The expression on her face when she found the first egg is something I'll never forget.

I launched my line of organic jams, and focused fully on the farm for the first time. Styling began to fall to the side, but I was happy. It was, and is, hard to let go of that life, and I still take the odd job just to keep my hand in the mix. But now I have a new mix, and thanks to Lily, there is a wee pinch of cinnamon in our blueberry lavender jam.

I AM A FARMER ...

I can honestly say, I'm living the dream. I have a wonderful family and own a charming organic farm—Missing Goat Farm to be exact. I don't have the sheep or cow, but we do have the fancy feathered fowl.

We are not die-hard organics, and some nights we still get our food from a can. We love sugary treats and chocolate. Doughnuts and crackers. We just discovered how fun it is when we make these things instead of buying them. There is a joy there that Lily will hold on to forever. She will teach her children and I will be called Grandma in her stories. Grandma made the best tomato soup, or, these were the cheese crackers Grandma made on a rainy day to make me smile. She will teach her children what I have taught her.

Being in the kitchen with a toddler can teach you many things. Patience for one thing. That perfection is highly over-rated. Sometimes things just go wrong. Accidents will always happen. And that a good dustbuster is really important to own.

Last summer, I did an interview for a pretty big newspaper who got wind of our sweet organic farm and line of jams. The story came out and everyone saw it. I remember reading it, then re-reading it. It was there in a national newspaper, so it must be true!

They called me, Heather Cameron the stylist/story producer ... a farmer.

Right off the bat, let me clear up a few things:
• You don't have to have children to enjoy this book.
• The recipes are for everyone.
• I am not a complete health nut or world famous chef. I am a mom and the owner of a small organic farm.
• I am a huge supporter of organic food choices, but do not push this on anyone.
• I like to eat well, but there are also times when I can't resist the bubbly goodness of a minty sweet chocolate bar.

We have an agreement in our neighborhood. At any time, any of us are allowed to wander about our yards in our pajamas. No one will mention it. I love this rule!

I also wanted to say, that even though I am a magazine stylist, I wanted this book to feel like my home. Not overly posed or propped. Just comfortable and light. I was so flattered to be asked to use my own photos. Over-the-moon happy. Having them alongside those by my dear friends Kim and Janis—who shoot stunning images with little or no effort—is beyond dreamy.

So, I hope you enjoy what I have created. I hope it feels fun and completely do-able.

And yes, we are wearing pajamas in a few shots.

MY LEARNING CURVE ...

When Lily became big enough to eat a full meal, I tried to be one of those brilliant moms who secretly put three extra puréed vegetables in every recipe. Problem was, I always got caught.

The choc chip chickpea cookies sat there, unwanted. The macaroni tasted thick. The cake smelled funny. My girl would say in as nice a way possible, "Mommy, this tastes a bit like maybe some dirt got in the bowl."

She was right. It did taste bad. So out went the frozen bags of green, white, and all shades of yellow. In came bags of frozen mango, coconut milk, kiwifruits, and bananas. Same colors I realize, but now I didn't have to worry about the day she could read the bags labeled cauliflower or peas. I brought in food that I wasn't trying to hide and I didn't have to worry about being exposed. I freeze it because she loves it. We all love it.

This book is simply about taking the time to go old school. Knead the bread by hand. Roll out the pastry dough you made from scratch. Whip up some butter—just so you can say you did. Even if you spend hours trying to make something and in the end it hits the trash bin. Who cares?

If you do it with a friend or with your kids, the memories make it worthwhile. The few hours you spend cooking, laughing, and then hating what you just made are brilliant. Irreplaceable.

I get notes from people all the time saying they have the best memories of making pasta with their grandmother. The whole family would gather, the pasta would be hanging from every part of the house, and the entire day was spent in the kitchen with the people you love.

Oh, and I must confess, I do slip one thing into her food still ... spinach. I put it in our smoothies and tell her it's kale. She loves kale, hates spinach. Not that she has ever tried spinach.

Why did we move so far away from this style of life? We got busy. I know. I'm busy.

If my girl wants to help make a meal, then I'm happy to have her by my side. We are together.

LILY AND HER LADIES ...

From the moment I brought five wee chickens home, all of 72 hours old, Lily was their momma. She loves animals, and taking care of these girls teaches her responsibility and appreciation of the birds. We make them mash on rainy days and sundaes when it snows. They give us beautiful eggs with yolks so orange, it's shocking.

MEET THE LADIES

In Lily's hands: Peep, a Buff Orpington.
Beside her: Lola, an Ameruacana and, truth be told, our favorite.
Below left: Haddie Doe, a Silver-Laced Wyandotte, named by Lily.
Below middle: Johnny Drama, because she seemed so full of herself and it rhymed with Brahma—which she is.
Below right: Cocoa, a cuckoo maran breed from France—so the name fits.

If Lily had her way, they would be called Crystal, Pink Purple Diamond—yes that's all one name—Glitterific, Flitter Fairy, and Princess Shimmer.

I always knew that I would love having chickens. We bought organic eggs in the past and thought their color so rich and yellow. Then we saw how orange our girls eggs were!

SPRING

FOR BREAKFAST
French toast
Savory cornmeal
    waffles
Smoothies

AS A SNACK
Choc chip granola bar
No-cook granola bar
Cheese crackers
Rhubarb and rosemary jam
Kale chips
Nachos with salsa cups
Broccoli soup
Bread-making
Homemade breadsticks

FOR A MAIN MEAL
Individual filo tarts
Pizza dough
Basic pizza sauce
Pasta from scratch
Chicken and veggie wrap
    with quinoa

FOR DESSERT
Banana mango mock
    ice cream
Meyer lemon curd
Meringue tarts
Pavlova clouds on vanilla
    pudding
Rhubarb pie

FOR THE PANTRY
Almond butter
Almond milk
Garlic scape pesto

Everything is coming back to life in the garden...

anything could happen this year.

LOVE... Spring!

Spring is when I get really motivated. Everything comes back to life, including me. Garlic and rhubarb are really popping up, as are the kale, spinach, radish, broccolini (baby broccoli), and lettuce. I use a lot of these in my spring recipes—along with mangoes. They are in season right now, and we love them so! By late spring, we are snapping off the garlic scapes (the tall flower that grows up the center of the stalk) and making pesto for the freezer.

The chickens start to lay again, so we get, on average, four fabulously fresh eggs a day. The girls are allowed to free range the property to eat up bugs and any baby slugs that may be eyeing our garden.

After a winter of planning and prepping our vegetable beds, it's exciting to see things pushing through the soil. The whole year is ahead, and you never know what is coming your way.

FRENCH TOAST

We have French toast often—silly often. I use the same basic recipe, but change the details. I choose fancy brioche or your average sandwich bread. Sometimes I spread cream cheese on them, other times yogurt. Fresh fruit—yes please!

MAKES ABOUT 4 SLICES

2 eggs
1 teaspoon ground cinnamon
2 teaspoons vanilla extract
⅓ cup (80 ml) milk
4 slices of bread (you choose: brioche, white, brown etc.)
Butter, for the frying pan–because it makes it taste so much better

1 Whisk the eggs, cinnamon, vanilla extract, and milk together in a shallow dish. Dip each piece of bread in the whisked mixture and then place in the buttery frying pan. Brown the bread on each side.

2 You can now either go for the classic butter and maple syrup combo or use some honey cinnamon butter (see recipe below.) You can also spread on some cream cheese and stuff fresh fruit between two slices. (A tip to make cream cheese more spreadable: melt it in the microwave for 10 seconds.)

HONEY CINNAMON BUTTER
¼ cup (60 g) butter, at room temperature
¼ cup (70 g) honey
1 tablespoon ground cinnamon
Mix all the ingredients together until blended and then spread on French toast, pancakes, or waffles. Any extra can be stored in the fridge for later use.

SAVORY CORNMEAL WAFFLES

I love waffles—but let's be honest, they're a lot of effort. Three bowls, beaten egg whites, folding... I've almost lost interest. But they're good—really, really good. The best way I have found to make the work worthwhile is to double the batch and freeze some for another day.

MAKES ABOUT 4 WAFFLES

1½ cups (200 g) all-purpose (plain) flour

¼ cup (35 g) cornmeal (polenta) or ¼ cup (35 g) all-purpose (plain) flour

1 teaspoon baking powder

½ teaspoon baking soda (bicarbonate of soda)

1 teaspoon salt

2 eggs, separated

2 tablespoons superfine (caster) sugar

½ cup (100 g) melted butter

2 cups buttermilk–if you don't have this, just add 2 tablespoons vinegar to 2 cups (500 ml) milk and let sit for five minutes

2 teaspoons vanilla extract

Topping ideas: fresh spinach, turkey bacon, fried egg, chives, cilantro (coriander), salsa, avocado, tomato

1 Mix the flour, cornmeal (polenta) or flour, baking powder, baking soda (bicarbonate of soda), and salt in a large bowl.

2 In another bowl, beat the egg whites until stiff. Add the sugar and beat until the peaks are shiny.

3 Mix the egg yolks, melted butter, buttermilk, and vanilla in a third bowl. Pour this into the dried ingredients and mix well. Fold in the beaten egg whites.

4 Cook in your waffle maker according to the manufacturer's instructions.

5 Now you can add your toppings of choice. I add spinach, a fried or poached egg, some turkey bacon, chives, and pepper. Have fun with them.

This recipe is for a savory waffle made with cornmeal but you can ditch the cornmeal and make a basic waffle batter instead. I must confess we have eaten these at dinner time, too.

We have a smoothie almost every day. Sometimes I add bee pollen (1 teaspoon) for an extra boost. It's so good for you, but follow the instructions and introduce it slowly to avoid any allergic reaction.

SMOOTHIES

I freeze smoothie ingredients all year. When a fruit I like is on sale, I buy en masse. I freeze sliced perfect bananas for smoothies and ice cream—not the brown old kind, I find they taste too, well, banana-y. Kiwifruits can be mashed into ice cube trays along with organic coconut milk when it's on sale.

I can't stress enough how much easier your life can be if you take the time to chop up the fruit and freeze it on a baking sheet first. I have tried far too many times to chisel apart mango chunks or chop off the peel from a frozen banana. So be smarter than that. Chop, pre-freeze, and then bag. The exception is blueberries. Those I dump straight into bags.

The spinach in this smoothie is almost undetectable if you add only one small handful. (If you are a grown-up, you can add more.) You can also add any protein powders or other fruits to this. It's a recipe that can be built upon or edited. Smoothies are pretty forgiving and fun to play around with.

FRUIT SMOOTHIE
MAKES 4

2 cups (500 ml) Almond Milk (page 50) or orange juice
1 cup (125 g) fresh or frozen blueberries
4 tablespoons plain or vanilla yogurt
1 banana
1 kiwifruit
A handful of fresh or frozen spinach (optional)
Agave nectar or runny honey may be needed to sweeten if using plain
    yogurt (optional)

Put all the ingredients in a food processor or blender and blitz until smooth. Serve immediately in tall glasses.

MANGO SMOOTHIE
MAKES 4

½ a fresh or frozen mango–heck, you can even use the whole thing
¼ cup (60 ml) fresh or 2 cubes of frozen coconut milk
2 cups (500 ml) pineapple juice
1 banana
2 tablespoons plain or vanilla yogurt
A handful of fresh or frozen spinach (optional)

Put all the ingredients in a food processor or blender and blitz until smooth. You can add spinach to this too. It makes it the most lovely shade of green, but then the kids spot it easily.

CHOC CHIP GRANOLA BAR

Ok, this bar has a few health qualities snuck into it, but the chocolate chips make it a treat. No one would ever know but you, so serve them with a smile and eat three for yourself.

MAKES ABOUT 20

2 cups (200 g) quick-cook oats
1 cup (130 g) wholewheat flour
¾ cup (150 g) brown sugar
1 cup (160 g) chocolate chips
½ cup (70 g) sunflower seeds
¼ cup (25 g) ground flax seeds
½ teaspoon ground cinnamon
½ teaspoon salt
¼ cup (70 g) runny honey
1 egg
¼ cup (60 ml) vegetable oil
2 teaspoons vanilla extract

1 Preheat the oven to 350°F/180°C/Gas 4 and line a 9 x 13 inch (23 x 33 cm) shallow baking tray with sides with parchment (greaseproof) paper.

2 Combine the oats, flour, sugar, chocolate chips, sunflower seeds, flax seeds, cinnamon, and salt together in a bowl.

3 In another bowl, mix together the honey, egg, vegetable oil, and vanilla extract. Pour this into the dry ingredients and mix well.

4 Spoon the mixture into the prepared baking tray. Press the mixture down firmly into the corners and bake in the preheated oven for 18–20 minutes. When you have slightly brown edges, remove from the oven. Those are my favorite parts as they are crunchy.

5 Use a large knife to cut the bake into bars while warm (the bars tend to crumble if you wait until they are cool to cut them.)

NO-COOK GRANOLA BAR

These taste like a version of a rice crispy bar, but have far less sugar and some healthy hemp seeds in them. Everyone who eats them, loves them. Plus, no oven required! If I were you, I'd double the batch as these will go fast.

MAKES ABOUT 12 BARS OR 20 SMALL ONES DEPENDING ON HOW BIG OR SMALL YOU CUT THEM

¼ cup (60 g) butter
⅓ cup (70 g) brown sugar
1/4 cup (70 g) runny honey
1 teaspoon vanilla extract
1½ cup (45 g) brown rice crispy cereal
½ cup (45 g) quick-cook oats (the slow cook will be tougher to chew as these aren't baked in the oven—I tried both, and really noticed a difference between the two bars)
⅛ cup (15 g) hemp seeds
Milk or dark chocolate, for drizzling (optional for you, but not for me)

1 Melt the butter, sugar, and honey in a saucepan over medium heat. Bring to a gentle boil and reduce the heat to a simmer. Simmer for 2 minutes and then remove from the heat and add the vanilla.

2 In another bowl, mix the dry ingredients together. Pour the butter mixture over the dry ingredients and toss well with a spoon.

3 Line an 8 x 9 in (20 x 23 cm) baking tray with sides with parchment (greaseproof) paper. It is easy to shape, so you can use a larger baking tray if needed; it won't run out of place. Press the granola into the pan firmly with your hands. If you rub a little butter on your hands it will stop the mix from sticking to you. Be sure it's pressed down well.

4 You can now melt the chocolate and drizzle it over the top of the granola mixture. Let it sit for about 15 minutes and then cut it into bar-size pieces. It cuts better when it's still warm. Once it's cut, you can let the bars set ... or dig in.

CHEESE CRACKERS

These are really best when they are warm from the oven, so I only bake half the recipe and throw the other half in the freezer for another day. I love having stuff for back up when I'm feeling uninspired or rushed.

MAKES ABOUT 40 CRACKERS

8 oz (250 g) Cheddar cheese, grated
5 tablespoons cold butter
1 cup (130 g) all-purpose (plain) flour

1 Place all the ingredients in a food processor or blender and blitz until everything binds together. It takes about a minute.

2 Remove the dough and mold it into a ball with your hands. This is where you can divide the dough and place half in the freezer or not if you have friends over or are cooking for a large family. Wrap up the dough with plastic wrap (clingfilm) and place in the fridge for one hour or overnight. Preheat the oven to 375°F/190°C/Gas 5.

3 Roll out the dough on a lightly floured surface—just under a ½ in (1 cm) thick, but you can experiment with thinner or thicker crackers. Cut out rounds using cookie cutters and place the shapes on parchment (greaseproof) paper on a baking sheet.

4 Another option is to take your pizza cutter and cut the dough into squares. It's superfast and kids like doing this.

5 Bake in the preheated oven for 8–10 minutes. Check them at 8 minutes—they should be just slightly brown on the edges. Too much and they can get a little dry tasting.

RHUBARB AND ROSEMARY JAM

I make this in the spring and sell it in the city. It goes fast as there is a serious love of rhubarb out there. It's the perfect little appetizer served with cheese. Also great on a warm croissant or mixed in yogurt!

MAKES ABOUT 2 JARS

1½ lb (750 g) sliced fresh or frozen rhubarb
1½ cups (500 g) granulated sugar
Juice of 1 lemon
¼ cup (70 g) runny honey
10 fresh rosemary sprigs or more (depends on how much you like rosemary)
Freshly ground black pepper (about 5 turns of the pepper mill)

1 Mix the rhubarb, sugar, lemon juice, and some black pepper together in a saucepan. Set over medium heat and bring to a boil, stirring constantly. Reduce the heat to medium to low and simmer for 6 minutes.

2 Add the honey and rosemary and simmer gently for another 6 minutes. Keep stirring as it likes to stick and spit if you don't.

3 Chill the jam and pour it into clean, sterilized jars. Serve it with goat's cheese or cream cheese and crackers. It's also good added to the top of a warmed brie wheel. It's even good on grilled cheese sandwiches, especially with thin slices of pear.

KALE CHIPS

I can't tell you how much we love these. They call for a dehydrator, which you can get at department or kitchen stores. I use mine to dry fruits, make roll-ups, and many other things. You could use the oven on a really low temperature, but I find the chips don't taste as good.

MAKES PLENTY OF KALE CHIPS FOR ONE SITTING!

⅓ cup (65 ml) tahini

¼ cup (60 ml) tamari (soy sauce)

¼ cup (60 ml) apple cider vinegar

½ cup (120 ml) water

Juice of 1 lemon

¼ cup (60 ml) nutritional yeast (available in most grocery stores or health stores)

2 large bunches of fresh kale (green, purple, curly, or less curly)

1 Place all the ingredients, except the kale, in a food processor or blender and blitz until smooth. Pour into a large bowl.

2 Wash your kale, and don't worry about drying the leaves, just give them a shake. Tear the kale into small pieces, or leave the leaves whole. Dip the leaves in the mixture, but try not to over-coat them (too much of the sauce can be overpowering.) Place the coated leaves on the trays of a dehydrator.

3 Turn the dehydrator on and leave it to run for about 4–6 hours. The time will depend on the size of your kale.

4 Once the kale leaves are super-dry and very brittle, they are ready to eat. Take them off the trays when they are warm—they will stick if you wait for them to cool. Store any leftovers in a large ziplock bag and seal.

*VANITY NOTE—this is not a food you want to eat on say, a date or with someone you are trying to impress. This is something, that after you eat, you must go straight to a mirror and check your teeth.

NACHOS WITH SALSA CUPS

This is super-simple and super-tasty. You can customize cups for each person, or make one large batch for everyone to share. My girl likes avocado with mango and basil. I like everything tossed together. You can add your favorite spring vegetables.

A GOOD SNACK FOR 3–4 EASY EATERS OR 2 REALLY HUNGRY ONES

1 large bag of tortilla chips
About 1–2 cups (200 g) Cheddar cheese, grated
  (depending of course on whether you intend to eat the whole bag or not)
1 avocado, peeled, stoned, and chopped
1 mango, peeled, stoned, and chopped
1 red and yellow pepper, deseeded, and chopped
A handful of fresh cilantro (coriander) or basil, chopped
8 baby sweet tomatoes, quartered

1 Preheat the oven to 325°F/160°C/Gas 3.

2 Place the tortillas on a baking sheet and sprinkle with the cheese. Bake in the preheated oven for about 6–7 minutes until the cheese has melted and is beginning to bubble.

3 Mix all of the remaining fresh ingredients together in a large bowl, or make individual salsa cups for everyone. You could also get each person to make their own cup. Having a lid makes it easy to close it up and give a good mixing shake. Serve with the chips to scoop oout.

Variation: you could also add some cooked black beans or sliced or chopped radishes to the salsa.

BROCCOLI SOUP

This soup puts a big smile on my face. What I love even more, is that it makes my daughter smile too. It warms you up, fills you up, and this soup is so darn good. If I had a store, I would serve nothing but soup and warm pie, and this is one of the soups I would serve. You can serve it with the Homemade Breadsticks on page 35 for a light lunch.

SERVES 4

5 cups (1.2 litres) vegetable stock
6–7 cups (375–400 g) broccoli (about 3 big heads), cut into bite-sized florets
1 tablespoon butter
2 medium or 1 large leek, sliced thinly
6–7 stems of kale, chopped
½ teaspoon dried thyme or 1 teaspoon fresh thyme
1 cup (250 ml) milk
1 cup (350 ml) heavy (double) cream
1 cup (90 g) Cheddar cheese, grated
Freshly ground black pepper, to taste

1 Heat the vegetable stock until simmering, then add the broccoli. Cook for about 10 minutes.

2 Melt the butter in a frying pan and sauté the leeks until soft and slightly browned. Add the leeks to the broccoli and stock.

3 Add the chopped kale and dried or fresh thyme and simmer for about 2 minutes until wilted and soft.

4 Transfer the soup to a food processor or blender and blitz until smooth. Pour the soup back into the saucepan and add the milk, cream, and cheese. Stir well and season to taste.

Topping suggestions: cooked quinoa, grated Cheddar cheese, crumbled blue cheese, croutons, goldfish (crackers).

BREAD-MAKING

This is a form of art. It's frustrating, it changes each time, the dough is sticky and my dishcloth becomes globbed with glue-like bits. But ... I promise, each time you will learn something. Each time, it will get better. Use these basic steps to make your dough for the Breadsticks (opposite), the Pizza Dough on page 38, and the Yummy White Baguettes on page 118. Ingredients are as listed for those recipes.

1 Put the flour and salt in a large mixing bowl and whisk together. In another bowl, combine the water and yeast. Let it sit a minute, then whisk well and pour into the center of the flour mix.

2 Use a pastry scraper to mix together lightly—you are not trying to blend it all together and make a ball, just get it to bind a bit. Tip the dough out onto a dry work surface. It is going to look like a gooey mess; this is good—do not add more flour. You must work the dough and it will come together. Too much flour and it will become tough. You also don't add flour to your work surface because it will be incorporated into the dough (again, the dough will become tough.)

3 Using your hands, fold the dough over onto itself, away from your body. Pull the dough up, then slap it down on top of itself. Keep folding and slapping down the dough. It will be very sticky, but as you work the dough, it will begin to bind together. This is a different version of the classic knead. This fold over style fills your dough with beautiful air and makes it light and lovely. Continue kneading for about 10 minutes.

4 Sprinkle a bit of flour into the mixing bowl and place the dough in it. Cover with a clean tea towel or your bread cloth. The dough needs to rest for one hour in a warm area of your kitchen.

5 Then use your pastry scraper gently to remove the dough from the bowl. It will feel soft and pillowy.

HOMEMADE BREADSTICKS

Follow steps 1 to 5, opposite, to make the dough. These breadsticks use the same technique in the beginning, but don't have to rise or rest for as long.

MAKES ABOUT 12 THIN BREADSTICKS (YOU CAN MAKE THEM FATTER IF YOU PREFER)

2½ cups (350 g) white bread flour
½ teaspoon salt
Scant 1 cup (225 ml) warm water
1 teaspoon traditional dried yeast
Olive oil
Sesame seeds (black or white), fresh herbs such as rosemary or thyme (optional)

Follow the same directions for making bread—but here you are making half the recipe.

1 After the first hour of rest/rising, remove the dough from the bowl. Shape the dough gently into a rectangle. Try not to pop any of the bubbles—these are beautiful and will make the bread heavenly.

2 Fold one-third of the dough over to the center of the rectangle and then fold the other third of the dough to the center. Take your pastry cutter and cut the dough into about 10–12 slices. Pick up each piece and gently twist.

3 At this point, you can drizzle on olive oil and dip the breadsticks in seeds or fresh herbs, if you like, or leave them plain. I do half and half because my girl doesn't care for seeds.

4 Place the dough sticks on a baking tray lined with parchment (greaseproof) paper and bake in the preheated oven for 10 minutes. Serve right away with Broccoli Soup (page 32) or any soup you are having.

NOTE: There are a few items that will help with this recipe: a plastic dough scraper and some 100% cotton tea towels designated for bread making only—you can buy specific bread cloths (they are very lightweight tea towels.)

INDIVIDUAL FILO TARTS

This family loves filo—but who doesn't? What this family doesn't love is the same fillings and vegetables. So, I've solved that by making individual filo tarts in small ramekin dishes. Put what you like in your own tart—cheese, veggies, meats ... up to you. Here is a suggestion to start.

MAKES 4 TARTS

1 package of filo pastry, at room temperature
¼ cup (60 g) butter, melted
Sliced veggies of choice: peppers, tomatoes, kale, sugar peas, zucchini (courgette)
3 eggs
¼ cup (60 ml) heavy (double) cream
⅓ cup (35 g) ricotta
1 cup (90 g) Cheddar cheese, grated
Fresh basil or other herbs of choice
Fresh chives, snipped

1 Preheat the oven to 375°F/190°C/Gas 5.

2 Roll out your filo pastry and slice the sheets into squares measuring about 6 x 6 in (15 x 15 cm). You will need three squares per ramekin dish.

3 Tuck one filo square into a ramekin dish with the edges of the filo hanging over the sides. Use a pastry brush to brush the melted butter over the filo. Drop in another square of filo, placing it across the first piece, brush with butter, and repeat one more time. Do this with three more ramekin dishes.

4 Place your veggies in each of the ramekin dishes. You can alter each one to suit everyone's tastes. My girl likes kale and cheese. I like lots of mixed veggies. Use what you have on hand—anything goes.

5 In a bowl, whisk together the eggs, cream, ricotta, and Cheddar cheese. If you are using basil or another herb, throw that in too.

6 Pour the mixture into the ramekin dishes over the vegetables. Sprinkle chopped chives on top (but perhaps leave this out if you are cooking for kids).

7 Bake in the preheated oven for 15 minutes. The filo should be golden brown and the egg mixture should look cooked. If you are using fresh tomatoes, it may look like it needs to cook for longer, but don't let the filo burn. Let stand for 10 minutes before serving and the mixture will set more. They will be very hot so cool for longer before serving to kids.

PIZZA DOUGH

Read the kneading instructions and have a look at the images for bread-making on page 34. Pizza dough uses exactly the same method, but there is also olive oil in this recipe. Pizza is, by far, my daughter's favorite meal, so I make this dough a lot!

MAKES ENOUGH FOR 4 SMALL PIZZAS

4 cups (565 g) white bread flour
1 teaspoon salt
1½ cups (360 ml) warm water
2 teaspoons traditional dried yeast
5 tablespoons olive oil

1 Mix the flour and salt together in a large bowl. In a separate bowl, mix the warm water, yeast, and olive oil. Let sit for a minute or two and then whisk together. Pour this into the dry ingredients.

2 Follow the directions for making bread dough on page 34. After the dough has been left to rise for one hour, preheat the oven to 425°F/220°C/Gas 7.

3 Divide the dough into four equal pieces with your pastry cutter. Fold over the outside edges of each piece and press them into the center of the dough using your fingertips to form a ball shape. Repeat, tucking the edges into the middle about six times per ball.

4 Place each dough ball on a lightly floured surface and let rest, covered, for 10 minutes.

5 Now stretch the dough with your hands and let its weight pull it out. A rolling pin will push out all the beautiful bubbles that you have created. Once it gets big enough, lay it on a baking sheet lined with parchment (greaseproof) paper, and gently pull to make it bigger if needed. It should be about 8 x 10 inches (20 x 25 cm) in size, but you may like your pizza crust thinner or thicker.

6 Spread on your pizza sauce and top with some fresh basil and toppings of choice. Bake in the preheated oven for 10 minutes.

NOTE: Do not mix your salt in with the yeast—salt kills the yeast action and your bread will not rise well.

BASIC PIZZA SAUCE

Nothing worse than making pizza and discovering you forgot to buy the pizza sauce. I did this far too often for my family's liking, so I came up with my own easy sauce. I keep extra in the freezer for the next time I forget, as I don't like the canned type any more.

MAKES ENOUGH FOR 8 PIZZAS (STORE ANY EXTRA IN THE FREEZER FOR ANOTHER DAY)

1 small onion, chopped
2 garlic cloves, sliced
1 tablespoon butter
A handful of fresh basil
one 14 oz (400 g) can of the best canned tomatoes you can find (or about 7 medium to small fresh tomatoes)
¼ cup (35 g) raisins
Salt and freshly ground black pepper

1 Sauté the onion and garlic in a frying pan with the butter. When they are soft and slightly browned, put them into a food processor or blender.

2 Add the basil, tomatoes, and raisins and blitz until smooth. Add salt and pepper, and taste to check the seasoning. Add a pinch more salt if needed.

Notes:
• The raisins will give the sauce a bit of sweetness and be undetectable.
• If you are using fresh tomatoes, chop and core before adding them to the pan with the onions and garlic. Sauté until they are soft. Pour everything in the blender and blitz until smooth.

NOTE: You can roll the dough out by hand, but I've tried that and can honestly say I wouldn't make pasta any more if I didn't have a machine. You may be stronger than I am, so give it a try.

PASTA FROM SCRATCH

Pasta is like bread—it can frustrate you and make you a little crazy, but once you figure it out, it's not so bad. The first time, I tried doing the flour well on the work surface and, within seconds, my eggs slid out to the floor. Next time, I tried rolling it by hand. This is hard. I called my sister. She has a pasta machine. My next dough was a complete disaster—way too much flour and not enough eggs. There also seems to be a debate about what flour to use. I've tried them all, and I do like the Tipo 00 flour, but in the country, it's not easy to get. I have found that bread flour works pretty well, too. Now let me share what I've learnt through a series of errors ...

THIS MAKES ENOUGH PASTA FOR 4 EASY EATERS, OR 2 HUNGRY ONES.

2 cups (275 g) Tipo 00 flour also known as Type 00 (if you can't find this, and it's not easy, use white bread flour—I find regular flour not as light), plus 1 extra cup (130 g)

4 medium eggs

1 I use my very large bread-making bowls—I told you about the eggs hitting the floor and I don't want to deal with that again. Put the 2 cups (275 g) of flour in the bowl and make a well in the center. Crack the 4 eggs into the center of the flour. Using a fork, begin to blend the flour and eggs together. It will come together nicely and become a nice but slightly sticky ball of dough.

2 Turn the dough out on to your work surface. Begin to knead the extra cup of flour—¼ cup (35 g) at a time—into the dough. It will absorb the flour and get worked into the dough as you knead it. The dough will become firmer and not sticky at all. You really have to work the flour in, as sticky pasta can jam up your pasta maker. Knead your dough for at least 15 minutes until it becomes firm. If you poke it, it should spring back out.

3 Divide the dough into four balls. Begin to roll it through the widest part of the pasta maker—number 1 for my machine. Each time you feed the pasta sheet through, move up a number to make the pasta thinner. I stop at 6 (the second to last setting.) Then feed the pasta through the noodle (spaghetti) slicer to cut it into strips.

4 Now the pasta is ready to cook! Drop it into a large saucepan of salted boiling water (1 tablespoon salt to a large saucepan of water.) Or, you can store it in the fridge until the next day. We usually eat it all in one sitting, but sometimes there is a bit for lunch the next day.

CHICKEN AND VEGGIE WRAP WITH QUINOA

This wrap makes me feel good—it's healthy and full of flavor. You can add chicken or keep it vegetarian—up to you. We have an abundance of radish this time of year, so I try to use them up in wraps and salads. They look great, too.

MAKES ABOUT 4 WRAPS

Buy or make some good tortilla wraps (see page 62)

Cream cheese—you can use cream cheese with added pineapple, too

1 roast chicken breast, sliced

1 red or orange pepper, deseeded, and sliced

1 avocado, peeled, stoned, and sliced

6 radish, sliced

1 cup (170 g) cooked quinoa, any kind or color

1 mango, peeled, stoned, and sliced

Sprouts or lettuce

1 Lay your tortilla down and spread cream cheese over one half.

2 Lay the chicken down the center and then start piling the toppings on. Sprinkle on some quinoa at the end, and there you go. Roll this up and enjoy.

NOTE: I like to keep a batch of cooked quinoa in the fridge for sprinkling on various meals as it's a good source of protein. It's a great addition to soups, wraps, salads, or mixed with cottage cheese and fruit.

BANANA MANGO MOCK ICE CREAM

sometimes, in the spring, we have heatwaves. I keep bananas in the freezer for smoothies, but also for days like this. This is a mock ice cream (it contains no dairy) and I highly recommend playing around with it by trying lots of flavors.

SERVES 2-3

2 perfectly ripe frozen bananas, peel removed
Agave nectar, for sweetening
Vanilla paste
2 fresh or frozen mangoes

1 Place the frozen bananas in a food processor and blitz until they become creamy—like soft serve (soft whip) ice cream. Have a taste and add some agave nectar and a few teaspoons of vanilla paste to taste. Have another taste—so yummy, right?

2 Scoop all the banana out of the food processor and give it a clean. Add the frozen or fresh mango and blitz until smooth. Have a taste ... I know! I like to make 2 separate batches so I can swirl them together. Add agave nectar as needed or try other flavors, such as frozen coconut milk or even some cocoa.

3 This is meant to be eaten now, right after making. It doesn't keep so well and loses some of its charm.

MEYER LEMON CURD

If you love lemon, you will make this recipe and then send me a handwritten note saying thank you sweet lady for introducing me to Lemon Curd. You are welcome. Now go for a jog.

MAKES ABOUT 4 JARS

5 eggs
1½ cups (300 g) granulated sugar
1½ cups (360 ml) fresh Meyer lemon juice (available winter to spring)
1½ cups (375 g) unsalted butter, cubed
¼ teaspoon salt

1 Place the eggs, sugar, and lemon juice in a double boiler. If you don't have a double boiler use a large bowl on top of a large saucepan and hold the pan in place with an oven mitt on. Whisk until smooth and continue whisking for about 5–7 minutes, until the mixture thickens. Remove from the heat and stir in the cubed butter and salt. Stir until it melts. Voila!

2 At this point you can grab a spoon and enjoy, or ladle into jars to keep in the fridge for a few weeks. You can also let cool completely in the fridge and then use it in a pie or tart (opposite).

NOTE: I have tried making this with regular lemons, but found it is not as good. Meyer lemons are sweeter and have less bite. If you do use regular lemons, then you may want to add an extra ¼ cup (50 g) sugar.

MERINGUE TARTS

Now that you are in love with the previous recipe for Lemon Curd, you will make these tarts and then send me a note saying I am wicked as you have just eaten three of them—it's OK ... I did too!

MAKES 4 TARTS
1 jar (1 pint) Meyer Lemon Curd (see opposite) for filling

FOR THE MERINGUE:
4 egg whites (general rule of thumb for meringue is 1 egg white to ¼ cup (50 g) sugar)
1 cup (200 g) superfine (caster) sugar
1 teaspoon vanilla extract (see page 129)

FOR THE CRUMB CRUST:
1 ¼ cups (125 g) graham cracker (digestive biscuit) crumbs
¼ cup (50 g) granulated sugar
¼ cup (60 g) butter, melted

1 Preheat the oven to 350°F/180°C/Gas 4.

2 Beat the egg whites in a stand mixer or with a hand-held electric whisk until they begin to firm up. Slowly start to add the sugar. You may need to stop and scrape down the sides. Keep beating for about 15 minutes until the egg whites are firm and can stand up on their own and the sugar has dissolved completely. Fold in the vanilla extract.

3 Mix the crumb crust ingredients together in a bowl. Press the mixture firmly into individual, lined muffin pans or a pie plate—I used parchment (greaseproof) paper, because if you haven't noticed yet, I use it a lot.

4 Bake the crust in the preheated oven for about 10 minutes. Let the shells cool completely and then spoon in your lemon curd filling.

5 Pile the meringue high as you can on top of the lemon curd—simply because it's fun and looks very cool.

6 Bake the tarts in the oven for another 10 minutes, but keep your eye on them, so the meringue doesn't over-brown. Let cool and then devour.

PAVLOVA CLOUDS ON VANILLA PUDDING

This is for those days when the sky is not so blue; for those days when there are no fluffy white clouds in sight. The pavlova looks like the pillowy clouds of summer, and they are crispy on the outside and deliciously gooey on the inside. If you have never had vanilla pudding from scratch, you don't know what you are missing. These can be eaten together or apart ... and they will be!

SERVES ABOUT 4 WITH PLENTY OF CLOUDS FOR LATER

3 egg whites (don't let even a pinch of yolk get in there, they just won't work as well)
¾ cup (150 g) superfine (caster) sugar
1 teaspoon vanilla paste or extract (page 129)

FOR THE VANILLA PUDDING:

2 ½ cups (generous 1 pint) low-fat or whole milk
2 egg yolks (and in this case, I'm going to suggest you remove the white squiggly bits)
½ cup (100 g) granulated sugar
3 tablespoons cornstarch (cornflour)
1 whole vanilla bean (pod), cut in half

1 Preheat the oven to 250°F/120°C/Gas 1/2.

2 Beat the egg whites in a stand mixer or with a hand-held electric whisk until they begin to firm up. Slowly start to add the sugar. You may need to stop and scrape down the sides. Keep beating for about 15 minutes until the egg whites are firm and can stand up on their own and the sugar has dissolved completely.

3 Fold in the vanilla paste or extract—if you fold in the paste ever so slightly, you will have pretty streaks of vanilla seeds in the pavlova.

4 Dollop spoonfuls of the pavlova mixture onto 1–2 baking sheets lined with parchment (greaseproof) paper. You should get about 10–12 pavlova clouds, depending on the size you make them. Try to get them high and fluffy looking, but if the kids are doing it, let them just have fun with the shapes.

5 Bake in the preheated oven for 15–20 minutes until just slightly browned. Turn off the oven and let cool in the oven for about 30 minutes.

6 Meanwhile, make the vanilla pudding. Put 2 cups (480 ml) of the milk and the vanilla bean (pod) in a saucepan to warm—not boil or cook, just to warm. Stir in the sugar.

7 In a separate bowl, add the remaining milk. Add the cornstarch (cornflour) and egg yolks and whisk until smooth. Pour this into the warming milk and stir constantly until thickened and the sugar has dissolved.

8 Spoon the mixture into individual dishes. Serve the pudding warm or chilled with a pavlova cloud sitting on top.

NOTE: You can serve this pudding in pretty vintage dishes, if you like, or in one large dish—up to you.

RHUBARB PIE

I'm obsessed with pie. I'm also a pie snob. I admit it openly. I've never had a pie away from home that has made me swoon, but I'll keep searching. Please give this a try. There's a learning curve, but once you get it, you will become a pie snob, too. Then I'll send you a button for our club.

MAKES 8 SLICES

FOR THE CRUST:
1 cup (225 g) cold unsalted butter, cubed
2 ¼ cups (300 g) all-purpose (plain) flour
1 egg
3 tablespoons cold water
1 teaspoon sea salt
1 tablespoon heavy (double) cream
Sugar, for sprinkling

FOR THE FILLING:
3 cups (325 g) chopped fresh rhubarb
  (you will need about 7 lb (3.5 kg) of
  rhubarb–once you cut off the tops and
  bottoms, you should have about 3 cups)
1 cup (200 g) granulated sugar
4 tablespoons all-purpose (plain) flour
1 egg

1 Preheat the oven to 425°F/220°C/Gas 7.

To make the pastry
2 Drop the cold butter into a large bowl and add the flour.

3 Use a pastry cutter to chop into the butter—use your muscles and work it until the butter is the size of peas. Sure, you can use a machine to do this, but I have two issues with this: 1. The mixer always overworks the dough and your crust is not flakey. 2. The best pie you ever had didn't come from a mixer. Go old school; use your hands.

4 Once you have the butter cut into the flour, mix the egg, water, and sea salt in a small bowl and whisk together. Pour over the butter and flour mixture. Mix as well as you can with a fork, then use your hands to mix it, but just a bit. You are not looking to make a smooth ball of dough, just a loose flakey mixture.

5 Grab just over half the dough mix—it will be crumbly in spots, and you'll think, "This can't be right, she should be looking for her goat, not making

pie," but you will see. Pile the dough on top of a sheet of wax paper. Place a second sheet on top of the pile and press it down with your hands. Take your rolling pin and roll it out between the wax paper. Roll it fairly thin and wide enough to fit a glass Pyrex pie plate. I've tried all types of pie plates, and I tell you, this is the best. Don't go ceramic—it looks pretty but it doesn't cook properly, and who will remember your plate if your pie is to die for? No one. But if your pie sucks, they'll all say, "What a lovely pie plate you used." Hmm. Slowly peel off the top sheet. Lift the dough and wax sheet up, flip it over, and lay it on your pie plate. Gently peel off the second sheet. Press into the pie plate, trim off the excess (which can be added to the other dough for the top.) Hey, did you notice? No messy dough to scrape off your work surface!

To make the filling

6 Place the chopped rhubarb in a bowl. Add the sugar, flour, and egg; mix well. Spoon into the pastry shell you have just made.

7 Repeat the wax paper process with the other half of the dough and lay it on top of the rhubarb filling. Flip the dough over after you have rolled it out—the bottom is always fairly wrinkly. Peel this side off first, then flip it over and lay the wrinkly side down on the pie filling. This way, your pie's top shell is smooth. Trim off the excess dough. Give it a pinch around its sides and cut three slits in the top for the steam to escape.

8 And now, I reveal a secret—take some heavy (double) cream or milk, pour about a tablespoon into your palm, and pour over the pie surface. Smooth the cream out evenly over the top, there can be little pools here and there, and then sprinkle a little sugar on top.

9 Bake in the preheated oven for 10 minutes and then turn the temperature down to 350°F/180°C/ Gas 4 and cook for 25 minutes. Have a peak. You should have a slight browning to your crust—not too much, though.

10 And there you go. You did it. Optimum eating period for a pie is two hours after it's been removed from the oven (1½ hours if you're desperate.)

VARIATION:
BLUEBERRY FILLING
4 cups (500 g) fresh blueberries
Scant 1 cup (200 g) granulated sugar
5 tablespoons all-purpose (plain) flour

Place the blueberries in a bowl, and with a potato masher, crush just over half of them. Add the sugar and flour and mix well.

Pour the filling into your fabulously homemade pie crust and bake—same baking temperatures and times as above.

ALMOND BUTTER

This can be applied to any nut—you can even make your own peanut butter! Roasting the nuts will make this work beautifully.

MAKES 1 JAR
2 cups (260 g) raw almonds (skins off if preferred)

1 Preheat the oven to 350°F/180°C/Gas 4.

2 Spread the nuts out on a cookie sheet and roast in the preheated oven for 8–10 minutes until they are just slightly brown. Remove and let cool.

3 Pour the nuts into a food processor and blitz them up—you will need to stop the machine and scrape the nuts down a few times. Within 8 minutes or so, the oils will be released and the nuts will become very creamy. Grab a spatula and scrape into a jar with a lid. The butter will keep in the fridge for about two weeks.

ALMOND MILK

We have almond milk smoothies every morning. When I realized how much almond milk I was buying, it really surprised me. When I read the side ingredient panel, that surprised me even more.

MAKES ABOUT 2 CUPS (480 ML) ALMOND MILK
About 3 heaping tablespoons of almond butter (see above), but shop-bought will be perfectly fine
2 cups (500 ml) water
Agave nectar, runny honey or 2 medjool dates, to sweeten

1 Put the almond butter and water in a food processor or blender and blitz until creamy and smooth. You can strain the mixture through a fine sieve if you like, but I don't bother.

2 If you want to make the milk sweeter, add a few organic dates, some honey, or agave nectar, and blitz again. Taste and adjust to your own liking.

3 Pour over ice and enjoy, or use this to make a smoothie like we do (see page 25).

VARIATION:
CHOCOLATE ALMOND MILK
Add 1–2 tablespoons cocoa powder and some more sweetener or dates. It's up to you to taste and adjust ... everyone is different.

GARLIC SCAPE PESTO

If you are growing garlic, you will be able to snap off the scapes—the tall, curly, flower stem that comes up the center of each plant. These are edible and taste like a mild version of garlic.

MAKES 2 ICE-CUBE TRAYS

Large handful of garlic scapes (about 12)
1 tablespoon olive oil
Fresh basil or parsley

1 Throw a handful of garlic scapes in a food processor or blender. Add a tablespoon of olive oil and a handful of fresh herbs. Blitz until smooth. Scrape the sides down, add a bit more olive oil as needed, and blitz some more.

2 You can add a few spoonfuls of this pesto to some fresh salsa or pizza sauce, or use as pasta sauce. We put our pesto into ice-cube trays and freeze it. The cubes are then dropped into a freezer bag, ready to use when needed.

SUMMER

FOR BREAKFAST

Granola
Quinoa, fruit, and cottage cheese
Crepes

AS A SNACK

A picnic plate
Homemade tortillas
Cinnamon tortilla chips
Roasted garlic with herbs
Potato salad
Yam fries
Strawberry lemonade
Mojito
Homemade cocoa
Iced teas
Fruit waters

FOR A MAIN MEAL

Halibut with crunchy lemon topping
Salmon with blueberry chutney
Eggplant (aubergine) stacks
Quick pasta dish
Goat's cheese and caramelized onion
   ravioli
Sesame chicken wraps
Savory tart
Fish taco with homemade tortillas

FOR DESSERT

Popsicles
Blueberry sorbet
Banana chips for ice cream
Snow cone syrups
Pavlova
Damn brownie
Chocolate zucchini
   (courgette) cake
Fire pit baked apples
Barbecued peaches

FOR THE PANTRY

Saving peaches
Pistou
Oven-roasted
   tomatoes
Simple syrup
Five-minute
   easy jams

summer reminds us why we work so hard *on this little farm we love.*

LOVE... Summer!

Summer is a season of mild insanity, but it's really exciting. The farm is open and no matter where you go on the property, there is something growing that you can eat. The vegetable garden is overflowing and fresh berries are everywhere. We have designated Saturdays as zucchini (courgette)-give-away-day because we grow so many.

In summer we make flower bouquets daily, and forts and tipis in the backyard from sheets and bamboo. We get up early to paint pictures in the garden when it's cool, and stay up late by the fire pit trying to play the guitar and eating Baked Apples (see page 92).

We harvest and dry all our own lavender for the Missing Goat Blueberry with Lavender jam. Garlic is pulled early August and hung to dry in the greenhouse (the smell of fresh pulled garlic is fabulous.) I always invite friends to help and take pictures. You never know what is under the soil or how big the garlic bulb will be.

GRANOLA

I make granola all year round. It's crunchy and chewy and can be dressed up any way you please. If you make a basic granola, you can let guests or family pick their toppings. Then everyone is happy and there isn't a fight over the existence of raisins on the planet.

MAKES ABOUT 8 CUPS (875 G)

4 cups (560 g) slow-cook oats
1 cup (80 g) sliced almonds
1 cup (100 g) chopped pecans or hazelnuts
1 cup (140 g) sunflower seeds
¼ cup (25 g) ground flax seeds
⅓ cup (80 ml) vegetable oil
½ cup (140 g) runny honey

1 Preheat the oven to 300°F/150°C/Gas 2.

2 Mix the oats, nuts, and seeds together in a large bowl. Add the oil and then the honey and mix well, tossing together.

3 Spread the mixture out on two baking sheets lined with parchment (greaseproof) paper and bake in the preheated oven for 23–25 minutes. Remove from the oven and allow to cool on the sheet.

4 When the granola has cooled completely, lift the parchment (greaseproof) paper and pour the granola into a bag or container. I avoid closing up the bag or storing in an airtight container so that it stays crunchy.

Variations: You could also add toasted coconut, pumpkin seeds, raisins or craisins, hemp seeds, cashews, wheatgerm ... the list is endless.

QUINOA, FRUIT, AND COTTAGE CHEESE

This one is really for me. I don't eat a lot of dairy products, but I do love cottage cheese. When I'm short on time or just need a good pick-me-up snack for some energy, this is my go-to-food. It's really more a suggestion than a recipe. Use any fresh fruit you have or love, and if you don't like agave nectar, try honey or maple syrup. It's superfast and will get you through a slump.

SERVES ME!

½ cup (100 g) cottage cheese

½ cup (175 g) fresh mango, chopped into pieces or ½ cup (60 g) blueberries, strawberries, or raspberries (really use whatever fruit you like best)

A sprinkle of hemp heart seeds (I love the nutty taste of these, not to mention how good they are for you)

⅛ cup (20 g) cooked quinoa (another superfood)

Agave nectar, for drizzling

1 Throw all the ingredients into a bowl and drizzle with a little agave nectar.

CRÊPES

We eat crêpes all the time. The best thing about them is you can make a batch of batter and leave it in the fridge for a few days. They're so versatile that we will have crêpes for breakfast, lunch, and even dinner. They don't always have to be sweet—it's all about the filling. I find that sometimes, and I don't know why, the batter can either be too runny or a bit thicker than usual. It may depend on the size of eggs or just the temperature of the day. So adjust with a wee bit of extra flour or water if you see the need.

MAKES ABOUT 8

2 eggs
1 cup (130 g) all-purpose (plain) flour
¾ cup (180 ml) milk
¼ cup (60 ml) water
½ teaspoon good-quality vanilla extract
Butter or oil, for greasing

1 Put all of the ingredients in a food processor or blender and blitz until mixed. Pour into a jug or large bowl and refrigerate for at least one hour or overnight.

2 When you are ready to cook the crêpes, use a piece of paper towel to lightly grease a frying pan with a little butter or oil, and place over medium heat.

3 Pour in about ½ cup (120 ml) of the batter and lightly tip the pan to swirl the mix around so that it covers the base of the pan—the thinner the crêpe the better.

4 Use a spatula to lift the crêpe up slightly when the sides start to pull up and away from the pan. Peel the rest of the crêpe up with your hands and flip it over. It will need just a minute or two cooking time on each side. Repeat to use up all the batter.

Filling ideas: For breakfast, we add yogurt, fresh fruit, whipped cream, and a wee drizzle of real maple syrup, but you could use agave nectar or honey instead. You can fill your crêpes with anything—sautéed mushrooms with spinach, bacon and eggs, asparagus and cheese are all delicious.

A PICNIC PLATE

We make picnic plates all year round. To us, this simply means lots of different foods on one plate, eaten anywhere you choose—in the tipi, on the hammock, on the couch, or while sitting in the kiddie pool trying to cool down. This is one of our favorite combinations: yogurt cheese, figs with honey, edamame beans, roasted strawberries, and our homemade crackers.

MAKES ENOUGH FOR 2-3 PICNIC PLATES

FOR THE YOGURT CHEESE BALL:
1½ cups (320 g) plain yogurt

FOR THE ROASTED STRAWBERRIES:
2 cups (200 g) fresh strawberries, hulled and sliced in half or quarters if they are large
1 tablespoon balsamic vinegar
1-2 tablespoons superfine (caster) suga
r
3 fresh figs, sliced
Honey, for drizzling
2 cups (250 g) fresh or frozen edamame beans
Sea salt
Homemade Crackers (see page 150)–or use your favorite brand

1 To make a yogurt cheese ball, spoon the yogurt into about four layers of cheesecloth (muslin.) Bring the sides up and twist so you have a ball of yogurt. Gently press and squeeze so that all the liquid comes out of the yogurt. You can leave it to hang over a bowl in the fridge overnight or keep kneading the yogurt until it becomes dry. Let chill in the fridge. You now have a soft, spreadable cheese ball.

2 To roast the strawberries, preheat the oven to 325°F/160°C/Gas 3. Toss the strawberries with the balsamic vinegar in a bowl. Lay the strawberries on a baking sheet lined with parchment (greaseproof) paper and bake in the preheated oven for 20 minutes. Place the roasted strawberries in a bowl and sprinkle a tablespoon of sugar on them. Mix them around until the sugar melts and have a taste. If you want them sweeter, add another tablespoon of sugar. These strawberries are also good served over ice cream or on a piece of sponge cake with whipped cream.

3 Slice the figs and drizzle with as much honey as you wish.

4 Place fresh or frozen edamame beans in a saucepan of lightly salted boiling water. Boil for five minutes and then drain. Sprinkle with some really good-quality sea salt.

5 Assemble all the ingredients on your plates ... and there you have a perfect picnic plate! Serve with Strawberry Lemonade (see page 68).

HOMEMADE TORTILLAS

These tortillas are simply amazing—delicious and so easy to make. Use them for fish tacos (see page 81), burritos, quesadillas, or for oh-so-tasty cinnamon chips (see opposite). So, first, I will tell you how to make a tortilla and then I will tell you how to make the chips.

MAKES ABOUT 12

2 ½ cups (325 g) bread flour, plus
   extra for dusting
1 teaspoon baking powder
½ teaspoon salt
3 tablespoons vegetable shortening
¼ cup (60 g) butter, plus extra for
   greasing
1 cup (240 ml) warm water

1 Place all the ingredients in a food processor or blender and blitz until it forms one big ball. Remove and give it a knead on a lightly floured surface for a few minutes. Divide the dough into 12 balls (slightly bigger than golf-ball size.) Cover with a clean tea towel and let rest for 30 minutes.

2 Now, you can either roll them out by hand, or pick up an inexpensive tortilla press at a kitchen store. I have a press, but find that it doesn't make the tortillas thin enough for my liking. So, after pressing the ball, I use my hands to stretch the dough out as thin as it will go without tearing. You should be able to see through parts of the

tortilla. You will figure it out quickly when you see the reaction in the pan to the thinner tortilla.

3 Have a frying pan ready—I lightly grease mine with some butter—and it set over low to medium heat. Lay the tortilla in the hot pan. It will bubble up and brown quickly—about 1–2 minutes on each side will do.

4 You can have a meal with these, or make the cinnamon tortilla chips (see opposite.) I do both and use the extra the next day for snacking. You can keep these in the fridge for 2–3 days.

CINNAMON TORTILLA CHIPS

This recipe I just got lucky with. I had extra tortillas and wondered if I would get a nacho chip if I toasted them. My girl wanted a snack and something to dip in her yogurt. So, I added a bit of sugar and cinnamon. The whole family now loves these ... they are so good.

SERVES 1

1 fresh tortillas (or day or two old)
Melted butter
Granulated or superfine (caster), for sprinkling
Ground cinnamon, for sprinkling

TO SERVE:
Fresh fruit
Yogurt—plain, with honey, or flavored ... your call

1 Preheat the oven to 325°F/160°C/ Gas 3. Use a pastry brush to apply a wee coating of butter to the tortilla and sprinkle over a bit of sugar and cinnamon.

2 Use a knife or pizza cutter to slice up the tortilla like a pie—you should get 8 pieces or so. Place them on a baking sheet lined with parchment (greaseproof) paper.

3 Bake in the preheated oven for 7–8 minutes until slightly brown. To serve, pile on a platter with some yogurt and fresh fruit in the middle.

ROASTED GARLIC WITH HERBS

By July we are harvesting large, incredibly beautiful bulbs of garlic. I don't even know the variety we grow any more, but does it matter? It's just glorious garlic that tastes divine. We often roast a head or two in the campfire or the oven. It's super-easy and will always impress.

1 HEAD OF GARLIC WILL SERVE 3–4 LIGHT SNACKERS

Whole garlic heads—as many as you like
Olive oil
Fresh herbs—thyme, rosemary, oregano
Bread and butter, to serve

1 Preheat the oven to 350°F/180°C/Gas 4. A campfire will do, too!

2 Cut out a square of parchment (greaseproof) paper and lay it on top of a piece of foil (this will stop the garlic and foil touching.)

3 Use a knife to slice off the top of each bulb of garlic, so you have exposed the tip of each clove. Place the garlic on the parchment (greaseproof) paper with foil underneath. Pour over a tablespoon or so of olive oil and scatter over your herbs. Close up the paper and foil, and pinch the foil closed.

4 Bake in the preheated oven for 45 minutes or, if you have a campfire or fire pit going, place it out of the direct flame and let it roast for about 40–60 minutes. Turn the parcel often so all sides cook evenly.

5 Serve the roast garlic warm with bread and butter. Each clove will be soft and delicious and will spread easily.

NOTE: I am not a fan of foil touching my food. I find I'm forgetful enough as it is without foil tampering with my brain. Now ... wait, what was I saying? Oh, yes ...

POTATO SALAD

The perfect picnic food in the summer has to be potato salad. I've taken to throwing whatever is growing in the garden in the bowl. It's one of those meals that we can make almost entirely from the food we have on the farm and that's a good feeling.

SERVES 4–5

8–10 medium to small new potatoes
½ cup (100 g) mayonnaise
½ cup (100 g) plain yogurt
1 tablespoon apple cider vinegar
1 tablespoon superfine (caster) sugar
¼ teaspoon celery salt
¼ cup (30 g) shallot, finely minced
1 tablespoon butter
6 radish, chopped
Fresh peas if you have them (or chopped sugarsnap peas)
2–3 medium to small kale leaves, finely chopped
2 eggs, hard-boiled and chopped
¼ cup (40 g) cooked quinoa (optional)

1 Cook the potatoes in a saucepan of boiling water until soft.

2 While the potatoes are cooking, mix your mayonnaise, yogurt, apple cider vinegar, sugar, celery salt, and shallots together in a bowl and whisk them well. Place the mixture in the fridge until the potatoes are cooked.

3 Drain the potatoes and cut them up in the saucepan—using two knives makes this easier. Add the butter and gently toss until it melts and coats the potatoes. Pour the mayonnaise mixture over the top of the warm potatoes and again toss gently.

4 Add the chopped radish, peas, kale, and eggs and mix in well. If you are using the quinoa, you can sprinkle that on now, or serve it in a side dish as an optional extra.

i'm so pleased that Lily doesn't like these—that's one less person I have to share them with.

YAM FRIES

These, in my mind, should be under the Meal section. I could eat these forever. We have been making yam fries for over 20 years, since I was just a wee baby. But I never understood how restaurants got them so crispy—something was on the outside, they almost had a batter on them. It became an obsession of mine. Now, I know ... and now you know, too.

I could eat these on my own, but I try to share with my husband. I try to share... but always end up running across the lawn with the last of them.

SERVES 1-2

1 yam (In Canada a yam is the very deep orange-colored potato on the inside—not the pale yellow-colored one)
4 tablespoons cornstarch (cornflour) ... yes, this is the secret!
Olive oil
Salt

FOR CHIPOTLE MAYO DIP:

¼ cup (60 ml) mayonnaise
¼ cup (60 ml) plain yogurt or sour cream
1 tablespoon chipotle sauce (more if you like it hot and spicy)
Juice of ½ a lemon

1 Peel and cut the yam into slices. Cut into fries that are not too thick or too skinny ... just the happy place inbetween.

2 Place the yams in a large bowl filled with water and let soak for 1–2 hours and then drain.

3 Preheat the oven to 425°F/220°C/Gas 7.

4 Fill a plastic bag with the cornstarch (cornflour.) Drop in the fries and close up the top. Shake the yams about until they are covered with the cornstarch (cornflour.)

5 Pour them onto a baking sheet lined with parchment (greaseproof) paper. Drizzle over some olive oil and give them another toss about so they are covered equally in oil.

6 Now, don't crowd the fries. This sounds silly, but you need to lay the fries out side-by-side not touching each other. Touching interferes with the crispiness. I learnt this the hard way.

7 Bake one sheet at a time in the preheated oven for 15 minutes, flip them over, and then bake for another 8–10 minutes. Don't try to cook two trays in a convection oven at once ... failure!

8 While the fries are cooking, make the dip. Mix all the ingredients together in a bowl and set aside until needed.

9 Give the fries a gentle salting when they are hot out of the oven and serve with the chipotle dip.

STRAWBERRY LEMONADE

This drink is pink and pretty, and is a favorite around here. Plus we have so many strawberries that we need to find new uses for them.

SERVES 3–4

3 cups (1¾ pints) water
Juice of 2 lemons
½ cup (120 ml) Simple Syrup (page 97)
½ cup (50 g) fresh strawberries
4 slices of orange
Lots of ice

1 Place all the ingredients in a pitcher or large canning jar and stir or shake well. It can sit overnight or for the day in the fridge and will become more pink as it sits.

MOJITO

The secret to this perfect summer cocktail is to use simple syrup infused with mint—when you make the syrup, add 7–8 fresh mint leaves to the batch.

SERVES 3–4

Fresh mint leaves
1 shot of white rum
1 shot of lime juice
1 shot of Simple Syrup (page 97), mint-infused
Lots of ice
A long piece of fresh mint to act as a stir stick (optional)
Splash of soda water

1 Place a few mint leaves in the bottom of a 10 fl oz (300 ml) glass. Give them a muddle to release the flavor and scent.

2 Add the rum, lime juice, and mint-infused simple syrup. Drop in lots of ice, a few extra mint leaves or your mint swizzle stick, and top up with soda water.

HOMEMADE COCOA

Nothing could be easier than making your own hot chocolate. Honestly, you'll never buy a packaged mixture again, full of the endless ingredients that you can't pronounce. The powder mixture will last, so if you want just one cup today, store the rest in a jar. Are you ready ...

MAKES 4 CUPS

½ cup (50 g) cocoa powder—the best quality you can find
½ cup (100 g) superfine (caster) sugar
4 cups (1 liter) milk

1 Sift the cocoa into a bowl and then whisk together with the sugar. Once it is well mixed, you are done ... you have made cocoa mix. If you like your cocoa less sweet, use less sugar or more cocoa.

2 Heat the milk, and then stir in the powder mix.

3 Pour into the cups. For a very indulgent treat, top with Marshmallows (see page 121) and some chocolate shavings .

Variations: You can add a pinch of cinnamon or cayenne powder for a little spicy kick.

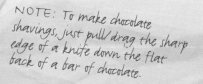

NOTE: To make chocolate shavings, just pull/drag the sharp edge of a knife down the flat back of a bar of chocolate.

ICED TEAS

I am a big fan of fruit water and fortunately we often have an abundance of fruits. We also have a lot of herbal teas, of which I'm not that fond, but when you turn them into iced teas, they are fabulous! These are super-easy to make and you can customize your own mix once you discover which blend you love the most.

MAKES AS MUCH AS YOU LIKE

Herbal teas, such as mango, passion fruit, berry blends
Fruits and/or herbs
Ice
Simple Syrup (see page 97) for sweetening

Choose a selection of the following, or pick your own favorites:
Peaches
Nectarines
Apples
Lemons
Oranges
Mint or rosemary

1 Make your tea on the weak side (too strong can be overwhelming,) then chill in the refrigerator. If you make a big pot of tea, you can always have some on hand for company or those extra hot days when water just isn't going to cut it. Store it in a sealed container in the fridge for later use.

2 Pour the tea into a large pitcher and add your fruits of choice, a few sprigs of mint or rosemary, lots of ice, and some of your Simple Syrup if you need to give it a bit of sweetness. Top up the pitcher with water if necessary. Stir well and serve.

Variations: With mango fruit tea I mix in sliced apples, nectarines, a few slices of lemon, and some mint. I also had a blend from Hawaii, to which I added peaches, oranges, and strawberries.

FRUIT WATERS

Fruits
Water
Ice

Choose a selection of the following, or pick your own favorites:
Cucumbers
Lemons
Apples
Cantaloupe
Water melon
Kiwi
Grapes

1 Chop up any blend of fruits and place in a pitcher. Fill with water and lots of ice—the fruit water should be very, very cold.

2 Serve all day or fill up your travel cup and hit the road, like I do. Everyone thinks I am drinking sangria! You can keep the waters in the fridge for one to two days but beyond that, the fruit will begin to fall apart.

HALIBUT WITH CRUNCHY LEMON TOPPING

You could do this with any white fish that you like—we just happen to love halibut. This recipe calls for preserved lemon, but if you don't have it, you can use the zest of a fresh lemon. I've also tried it with Panko breadcrumbs, but prefer the basic dried breadcrumbs.

SERVES 8–10

4 halibut steaks
4 thin slices of Preserved Lemon (see page 153) or grated lemon zest if preferred
¼ cup (60 g) butter, melted
2 cups (100 g) fresh or dried breadcrumbs
1 tablespoon fresh dill or ½ tablespoon of dried dill
A pinch of freshly ground black pepper

1 Preheat the oven to 350°F/180°C/Gas 4. Rinse the halibut steaks and place them on a baking sheet lined with parchment (greaseproof) paper.

2 Remove the pulp from the preserved lemon and just use the rind. Use a knife to chop and mash up the rind until it resembles a paste. Mix this into the melted butter.

3 Mix the breadcrumbs and melted lemon butter together in a bowl and add the dill and black pepper. Pile this onto your halibut steaks and sprinkle the lemon zest on top of each piece.

4 Bake in the preheated oven for about 20 minutes. This could vary depending on the size of your halibut steak, but the center should be light and flaky.

SALMON WITH BLUEBERRY CHUTNEY

We eat a lot of fish. Salmon is probably the most popular with everyone. A good salmon really doesn't need much done to it, but now and then, I love to add a dollop of blueberry chutney on the side. They really do have a sweet love affair with each other.

SERVES 4

1 salmon fillet, large enough for 4 people
4 tablespoons butter
1 lemon, sliced
Fresh dill, roughly chopped

FOR THE BLUEBERRY CHUTNEY:
3 cups (375 g) fresh or frozen blueberries
Grated zest and juice of 1 lemon
⅛ cup (20 g) red onion, minced
⅛ cup (30 ml) red wine vinegar
¼ cup (70 g) real maple syrup
¼ cup (50 g) brown sugar
¼ teaspoon ground ginger
¼ teaspoon ground cloves

1 Preheat the oven to 350°F/180°C/Gas 4.

2 Rinse the salmon fillet and lay it on a baking tray, skin-side down.

3 Brush the butter on top of the fish, then add the lemon slices and dill. Bake in the preheated oven for about 20–25 minutes (depending on the size of your fillet.) This can be done on the barbecue, if preferred.

4 Meanwhile, make the chutney. Place all the ingredients in a medium saucepan and bring to a boil, stirring well. Reduce the heat to a gentle simmer and continue to cook for 10 minutes, stirring often.

5 Serve the roasted salmon with the chutney on the side and some lovely fresh green vegetables.

NOTE: The blueberry chutney can be served warm or chilled with salmon, chicken, over a wheel of brie on sandwiches, or with cheese and crackers.

EGGPLANT (AUBERGINE) STACKS

This is a summer version of Eggplant (Aubergine) Parmesan (see page 143). It has similar fresh ingredients but isn't baked and covered in sauce. I added Pistou (see page 96) but you could add pesto or fresh basil instead. I could eat the baked eggplant (aubergine) slices on their own.

SERVES 4

1 eggplant (aubergine)
2 cups (150 g) breadcrumbs or Panko breadcrumbs
A pinch of salt and freshly ground black pepper
2 eggs, beaten
Vegetable oil
3–4 fresh tomatoes–the best you can find
2 large fresh buffalo mozzarella
4 tablespoons Pistou (see page 96)
Balsamic reduction

1 Preheat the oven to 350°F/180°C/Gas 4.

2 Slice the eggplant (aubergine) into thin circles about ½ in (1 cm) thick. Put the breadcrumbs in a shallow bowl, add a pinch of salt and pepper, and mix in well. Put the beaten egg in a separate shallow bowl.

3 Dip each slice of eggplant (aubergine) first in the beaten egg and then in the breadcrumbs. Lay them on a baking sheet lined with parchment (greaseproof) paper. Once they are all dipped and coated, drizzle vegetable oil over each piece.

4 Bake in the preheated oven for 20 minutes and then flip them over and bake for another 15–20 minutes. Remove and set aside.

5 Slice the tomatoes and mozzarella—they should all be equal thickness. You can stack these high or in one layer—it's up to you. Start with one eggplant (aubergine) slice, spread on a thin layer of Pistou sauce, then add your mozzarella, then tomato, and repeat until all of the eggplant (aubergine) has been used. Drizzle with a little balsamic reduction and you are done.

QUICK PASTA DISH

Make the pasta (see page 41) or buy a good-quality variety. You can add any sort of vegetable or herbs to this—kale, spinach, roasted zucchini (courgettes), toasted pine nuts—heck, add them all! It's a good base sauce to make and then use up what you have in the garden or fridge.

SERVES 3

Enough pasta for 3 people
½ cup (120 ml) heavy (double) cream
½ cup (70 g) Port Salut cheese (or your favorite melty cheese; I've used mozzarella and goat's cheese)
1 egg yolk
Freshly grated Parmesan, for sprinkling
1 cup (150 g) fresh or frozen peas or 1 cup (75 g) spinach
Toasted pine nuts, to serve

1 Bring a large saucepan of water to a boil, salt it well, add your pasta, and cook until al dente.

2 Put the cream and cheese in another saucepan. Warm over medium heat, stirring, until the cheese melts.

3 Drain the pasta once it is ready and return it to the pan. Pour over the melted cheese sauce and give it a good toss. Add the egg yolk and stir well—it will cook from the heat of the pasta and sauce.

4 Grate over some Parmesan and sprinkle over your fresh peas (if you are using frozen peas, you will need to cook them first). If you are using spinach, stir it in while the pasta is still hot so that it wilts.

5 Serve with extra Parmesan for sprinkling or toasted pine nuts.

GOAT'S CHEESE AND CARAMELIZED ONION RAVIOLI

I keep saying this, but I do believe this is one of my favorite meals. It's all about the filling, and let's face it, the pasta from scratch is pretty darn good, too. I picked up a very inexpensive ravioli maker in a store and it works perfectly for this recipe.

MAKES 48

1 yam
1 sweet onion, thinly sliced
2 tablespoons butter
¼ cup (50 g) goat's cheese
1 batch of fresh pasta dough (see page 41)

1 Preheat the oven to 375°F/190°C/Gas 5.

2 Wrap the yam in parchment (greaseproof) paper and then in foil and bake in the preheated oven for one hour. (You can do this the day before or earlier in the day, if you like.) Once baked, remove the peel from the yam, and mash the flesh.

3 While the yam is cooking, caramelize the onion in a frying pan with the butter—you want it to be brown and delicious. Once cooked, add the onions to the yam with the goat's cheese. Mix well.

4 Roll the fresh pasta dough sheets to a nice thin setting, but not so thin that it will tear when stretched. Sprinkle a bit of flour over your ravioli maker to make it easier to get them off. Lay the sheet of pasta over your ravioli maker. Spoon about one teaspoon of the filling over each hole. Once they are all filled, lay another sheet over the top. Gently press down. Get out your rolling pin and roll it over so the edges are sealed and cut. Now pull them off and lay on a sheet to dry while you make the rest.

6 Drop the ravioli in a saucepan of salted boiling water and cook for about five minutes.

Serving suggestions:
• You can serve the ravioli with a fresh or shop-bought tomato and basil sauce. We also like candied pecans with fresh basil and Parmesan.
• Another way is to lay the ravioli in a baking dish, pour a jar of tomato and basil sauce over the top, and bake in an oven preheated to 350°F/180°C/Gas 4 for about 25 minutes. Serve with Parmesan and candied pecans. Can you tell I really want you to try candied pecans?!

SESAME CHICKEN WRAPS

Sesame chicken or turkey is a staple for us. It's good plain, in wraps or on salad, or in this case, in lettuce. I mix in hemp seeds with the sesame seeds or sometimes use nutritional yeast. My daughter loves the nutritional yeast version best ... go figure!

SERVES 3–4 AS A LIGHT MEAL

FOR THE DRESSING:
¼ cup (50 g) tahini
A handful of cilantro (coriander)
½ avocado, chopped
Juice of 1 lime
1 teaspoon root ginger, freshly grated
⅛ cup (35 g) runny honey
½ cup (120 ml) water

FOR THE WRAPS:
2 boneless turkey or chicken breasts
½ cup (70 g) sesame seeds
Olive oil
2 tablespoons nutritional yeast or 2 tablespoons hemp
    seeds (optional)
Large lettuce leaves, washed, for wrapping
2 carrots, cut into thin sticks
1 small to medium cucumber, cut into thin sticks
½ cup (70 g) snow peas (mangetout), cut into thin sticks

1 To make the dressing, put all the ingredients in a food processor or blender and blitz until smooth. If it seems too thick, add a splash more water, but you don't want it to run out of your wrap. Set aside until needed.

2 Cut your chicken or turkey into strips so they will cook quickly and all the way through.

3 Put the sesame seeds in a small shallow bowl and mix in the yeast or hemp seeds, if using. Dip the meat in the seeds so that it is coated all over.

4 Heat a frying pan with the olive oil and add the meat. Fry on each side until just lightly browned and cooked through.

5 To assemble your wraps, lay the chicken on large lettuce leaves, add the vegetables, and pour the dressing over the top. Roll up and enjoy!

SAVORY TART

You can make this tart using the pastry recipe on page 48, or filo pastry, and again, it's a way to use up items from the garden or fridge. We make many versions of this tart all year round that reflect what is growing outside.

SERVES 4–6 AS A LIGHT MEAL

1 batch of pastry (see page 48)
1 onion, chopped
1 small zucchini (courgette), thinly sliced
A few zucchini (courgette) flowers, if you have them, sliced into 4
Fresh thyme leaves
2 apricots or 1 peach, peeled, and thinly sliced
½ cup (100 g) goat's cheese
Honey, to drizzle
Olive oil, to drizzle

1 Preheat the oven to 350°F/180°C/Gas 4.

2 Make your pastry following the instructions on page 48 and roll out half the dough on a piece of parchment (greaseproof) paper. Roll it into a rectangle about 7 x 10 in (18 x 25 cm) and keep it quite thin. Use a knife or pizza wheel to trim off the edges so you have a nice shaped rectangle (though rough shaped can look nice, too—shape it to make yourself happy ... sometimes my shape looks like a splat.)

3 Heat a little oil in a frying pan and fry the onion until caramelized. Sprinkle the onions over the pastry. Lay on the zucchini (courgette) slices, flowers, and the apricot or peach slices. Drop bits of the goat's cheese evenly over the top and then add a sprinkling of fresh thyme leaves. Drizzle honey and a little olive oil over the top.

4 Bake in the preheated oven for 25–30 minutes until the pastry is golden brown.

FISH TACO WITH HOMEMADE TORTILLAS

Any way to use homemade tortillas and I'm on it. I had a fish taco in Mexico once that I'll never forget, and this is as close as it gets to that memory. We like using two types of fish, such as halibut and trout. We mix the two fish together in the tortilla, or have them separate.

I have a tortilla press; I love it, but a rolling pin will work, too. Extra tortillas can be used for cinnamon chips (see page 63) or kept in the fridge for a few days and used for burritos or quesadillas.

SERVES 4

3 thin fillets of white fish, trout, or salmon, weighing about 15 ounces (475 g) in total
¼ cup (60 g) butter
1 slice of Preserved Lemon (see page 153), minced to a paste, or the grated zest of 1 lemon
¾ cup (55 g) breadcrumbs or Panko crumbs
1 batch of Homemade Tortillas (see page 62)
1 batch of Chipotle Mayo Dip (see page 67)

FOR THE SALSA:

6 radish, sliced
1 mango, peeled, stoned, and diced
½ avocado, chopped
Juice of ½ lime
A handful of cilantro (coriander), chopped
10 cherry tomatoes, quartered

1 Preheat the oven to 350°F/180°C/Gas 4.

2 Rinse the fish fillets and then lay them on a baking tray lined with parchment (greaseproof) paper.

3 Melt the butter in a small saucepan. Add the preserved lemon or grated lemon zest and the breadcrumbs or Panko crumbs, and mix well.

4 Sprinkle this crumb topping lightly over the fish and bake in the preheated oven for 20 minutes. If you have larger fish, it may take a bit longer. (You can pan fry the fish fillets in 1 tablespoon butter if preferred.)

5 While the fish is cooking, make the salsa. Toss all the ingredients together in a bowl.

6 To assemble the tacos, lay out a tortilla, add the fish in the center, spoon over some of the salsa, and then drizzle over some chipotle sauce. Roll up and eat with your hands.

NOTE: Making popsicles is one of our favorite things to do. We pick the fruit, run it through the food mill, and have popsicles made all within 30 minutes.

POPSICLES

For years we have made popsicles, but there is nothing worse than getting kids excited for popsicles, making them, and then telling the kids that they can have them tomorrow. Not good. So, I broke down and bought an instant popsicle maker. Ready in 7 minutes. Very good. We still do the overnight popsicles, and this will work any way you decide to freeze them. You will also need a food mill—they are not expensive and once you have one, you will find all sorts of uses for it.

**MAKES 6 LARGE POPSICLES
OR 12 SMALLER ONES**

4 cups (400 g) fresh fruit—strawberries,
   raspberries, blueberries ... your choice
1 quantity of Simple Syrup (see page 97)

1 Run your fresh fruit through the food mill. You will capture the skin and most seeds in the mill, while the juices go through to the bowl underneath.

2 Now it's time to add your Simple Syrup—it is entirely up to you to decide how much. I stand there with Lily and let her taste the mixture until she says "perfect!" Start with a ¼ cup (60 ml) and work your way up.

3 Once everyone is happy with the sweetness, pour the mixture into your popsicle molds and wait either 7 minutes or until the next day.

BLUEBERRY SORBET

Honestly, I think sorbet is just a popsicle in a container. Right? You will need the food mill again—didn't I tell you it would be handy. You will also need an ice-cream maker.

SERVES 3–4 IF YOU ARE DAINTY ABOUT IT

6–7 cups (750–875 g) fresh blueberries
½ cup (120 ml) water
1 cup (240 ml) Simple Syrup (see page 97)
Grated zest of 1 lemon

1 Run the blueberries through the food mill—you should get about 3 cups (1¼ pints) of liquid from them.

2 Add the remaining ingredients, mix, and then add to your ice-cream maker. Churn for 20 minutes or according to the manufacturer's instructions.

3 Eat it right away or transfer it to the freezer for later. It will harden up in the freezer, so remove it and let it sit for 30 minutes before serving.

VARIATION: STRAWBERRY OR RASPBERRY SORBET:

6–7 cups (750–875 g) fresh strawberries or raspberries
½ cup (120 ml) water
1 cup (240 ml) Simple Syrup (see page 97)

Run your berries through the food mill. Add the simple syrup and then pour into your ice-cream maker. Churn for about 20 minutes or according to the manufacturer's instructions.

BANANA CHIPS FOR ICE CREAM

This is a super-easy topper for ice cream in the summer time. These are like ready-made mini banana split accessories for your bowl. So when the kids think you are dull, serving vanilla ice cream, you can impress them with these.

SERVES 4

1 perfectly ripe banana
⅓ cup (60 g) milk or dark chocolate, melted
Milk, if needed
¼ cup (30 g) chopped pistachios,
    almonds, or hazelnuts ... your choice

1 Cut a perfectly ripe banana into thin slices. Lay the slices on a baking tray lined with parchment (greaseproof) paper.

2 Melt the chocolate in a glass bowl set over a saucepan of boiling water (making sure the base of the bowl does not touch the water.) I use organic chocolate and find that I always have to add a wee bit of milk to make the chocolate pourable.

3 Spoon a teaspoon or so of chocolate onto each banana slice. It's ok if it runs off. Sprinkle your chopped nuts of choice on top. Put the tray in the freezer for a few hours or overnight.

4 Once they are frozen, you can toss the slices in a container or ziplock bag to keep in the freezer.

SNOW CONE SYRUPS

Last of all, in the iced desserts section, I bring you the snow cone made with homemade syrups that you can feel good about. And, before you wander off thinking this is for kids, let me just say ... a shot of alcohol in a snow cone makes an instant summer cocktail. You will need a jelly bag strainer for this (found at any kitchen store and very inexpensive.) There is definitely something about the little pile of snow in a cup that makes you smile.

MAKES 1½ CUPS (360 ML) EACH SYRUP

PINEAPPLE SYRUP:
1 whole pineapple, peeled, cored, and cut into pieces
½ cup (120 ml) Simple Syrup (see page 97)
4 fresh mint leaves
Juice of 1 lime

BLUEBERRY SYRUP:
3 cups (375 g) blueberries
1 cup (240 ml) Simple Syrup (see page 97)
Grated zest and juice of ½ a lemon
½ cup (120 ml) water

STRAWBERRY SYRUP:
3 cups (300 g) strawberries
1 cup (240 ml) Simple Syrup (see page 97)
Juice of 1 lemon

RHUBARB SYRUP:
4 cups (400 g) rhubarb, cut into pieces
1½ cups (360 ml) Simple Syrup (see page 97)
1 fresh rosemary sprig

1 Choose which flavor syrup you are going to make. Put all the ingredients in a saucepan over medium heat and bring to a boil. Reduce the heat and simmer gently for five minutes, stirring from time to time.

2 Pour into a jelly bag strainer (or a strainer lined with cheesecloth/muslin) set over a bowl. Let the juice run through into the bowl below. When it cools to the touch, help force it through with a spoon.

3 Crush some ice in a snow-cone maker or in a blender. Pile into a bowl or cone and pour over any of these fantastic homemade syrups.

ADULT SNOW-CONE OPTIONS:
use less simple syrup with adult versions.
o Add ½ shot vodka to the cup with rhubarb-flavored syrup.
o Add ½ shot tequilla to the cup with strawberry-flavored syrup
o Add ½ shot rum to the cup with pineapple-flavored syrup, and an extra sprig of mint.

PAVLOVA

What happens when you have laying chickens and multiple varieties of fruit bushes in the same place? Pavlova happens. So easy, so impressive, so good. Crunchy on the outside, gooey on the inside ... you can't go wrong!

SERVE 4-8

4 egg whites
1 cup (200 g) superfine (caster) sugar
1 teaspoon vanilla paste or extract
Whipped cream and fresh fruit, to serve

1 Preheat the oven to 275°F/140°C/Gas 1.

2 Beat the egg whites in a stand mixer or with a hand-held electric whisk until they begin to firm up. Slowly start to add the sugar. You may need to stop and scrape down the sides. Keep beating for about 15 minutes until the egg whites are firm and can stand up on their own and the sugar has completely dissolved. Fold in the vanilla extract.

3 Scoop out the meringue onto a baking tray lined with parchment (greaseproof) paper, piling it about 4 in (10 cm) high in a circular shape.

4 Bake in the preheated oven for one hour. The meringue will have a slight golden tinge to it when it's done. Remove from the oven and let cool. As it cools, it will collapse and crack a bit—that is normal and to be expected.

5 Add some whipped cream to the top and cover with fresh fruit.

Variation: I sometimes add custard to the top under the whipped cream ... give it a try.

NOTE: If you have a big party with lots of guests, you can make multiple layers of pavlova and stack them on top of each other. You can also fold some cocoa into the meringue for a chocolate version.

DAMN BROWNIE

To me, a brownie should be chewy and gooey on the inside, but crunchy on the outside. The top should be crinkled and collapsed. If you have a true brownie, you don't need frosting. I call it damn brownie, because when you taste it, you will say "Damn, that's a good brownie."

MAKES ABOUT 16

¾ cup (175 g) salted butter, plus extra for greasing

1½ cups (300 g) granulated sugar

2 eggs

1 teaspoon vanilla extract

1¼ cups (175 g) all-purpose (plain) flour

¼ cup (25 g) cocoa powder

¼ teaspoon baking soda (bicarbonate of soda)

½ teaspoon baking powder

1 cup (175 g) milk chocolate, melted

⅛ cup (30 ml) milk

½ cup (60 g) toasted pecans, chopped (they must be toasted so they are crunchy)

3–4 marshmallows (I used the homemade kind, see page 121, but I'm sure shop-bought are delicious, too)

1 Preheat the oven to 350°F/180°C/Gas 4 and grease an 8 x 12 in (20 x 30 cm) baking pan.

2 Melt the butter and pour into a bowl. Add the sugar and beat with a hand-held electric mixer. Add the eggs and vanilla and beat well until it's smooth and creamy.

3 Sift the flour, cocoa, baking powder, and baking soda (bicarbonate of soda) together in another bowl and mix together. Add the butter mixture and stir together well.

4 Melt the chocolate in a bowl set over a saucepan of boiling water (making sure the base of the bowl doesn't touch the water.) I use organic chocolate and find that I need to add the milk to make it smooth—if your chocolate already seems smooth, skip the milk.

5 Pour the melted chocolate into the batter. Fold and blend it together. Mix in the toasted chopped pecans.

6 Pour the batter into the prepared baking pan. Tear each marshmallow into about three pieces and poke them into the batter so they are almost covered—some can be poking out on top and others buried deeper—keep it random.

7 Bake in the preheated oven for 30–35 minutes. Damn—these are good!

CHOCOLATE ZUCCHINI (COURGETTE) CAKE

There is much debate over this cake in our home. I like it because we have far too many zucchini in the summer. Lily likes it with cream and strawberries. My husband wants butter frosting on it. This makes perfect muffins too—great for when you're on the go or camping.

MAKES ABOUT 12 SLICES

2 ½ cups (325 g) all-purpose (plain) flour
½ cup (50 g) cocoa powder, sifted
3 teaspoons baking powder
1½ teaspoons baking soda (bicarbonate of soda)
1½ teaspoons salt
2 teaspoons ground cinnamon
¼ teaspoon ground nutmeg
2 cups (200 g) granulated sugar
1 cup (200 g) unsalted butter, at room temperature, plus extra for greasing
3 eggs
2 teaspoons vanilla extract
½ cup (120 ml) milk
⅓ cup (80 ml) Apple Sauce (see page 128)
2 cups (300 g) grated zucchini (courgette)
1 cup (175 g) milk chocolate, melted

1 Preheat the oven to 350°F/180°C/ Gas 4 and grease a 9 x 13 in (23 x 33 cm) cake pan or bundt pan.

2 Combine the flour, sifted cocoa, baking powder, baking soda (bicarbonate of soda,) salt, cinnamon, and nutmeg in a large bowl and mix together.

3 Beat the sugar and butter together in another bowl until light and creamy. Add the eggs and vanilla and beat until smooth.

4 Add the milk and apple sauce and continue beating. Pour this wet mixture into the flour bowl and blend together. Stir in the grated zucchini (courgettes,) pour in the melted chocolate, and stir again.

5 Pour the mixture into the prepared cake pan and bake in the preheated oven for 40 minutes. If using a bundt pan, it may take closer to 55 minutes.

6 Let your cake cool a little before removing it from the pan. Then put it on a wire cooling rack and let cool completely.

FIRE PIT BAKED APPLES

This is a perfect, easy, and ready-made dessert for camping or out around the fire pit. I like mine peeled as does my girl. The whole apple becomes a warm gooey delicious mess. You may prefer the peel left on. Do both so everyone is happy. We did. But they wished they asked for peeled after they tasted ours.

SERVES 2

2 apples
4 teaspoons brown sugar
1 teaspoon ground cinnamon
2 tablespoons butter

1 Preheat the oven to 350°F/180°C/Gas 4 if not cooking over the fire.

2 If you are going to try the peeled version—our favorite—then peel and core the apples. (I use a melon ball scoop to clean out the core of the apple, and we have an apple peeler—so handy, especially in the fall.)

3 Place the apples on a piece of parchment (greaseproof) paper that is laid on top of some foil.

4 Mix the brown sugar and cinnamon together in a small bowl and spoon into the center of each apple.

5 Place 1 tablespoon of butter on top of the sugar mixture and wrap up tightly in the parchment (greaseproof) paper and the foil.

6 Bake in the preheated oven for about 45 minutes, or take them out to the fire pit and place them by the hot coals. Turn every 20 minutes or so and leave them in for about an hour (it depends how hot your fire is.)

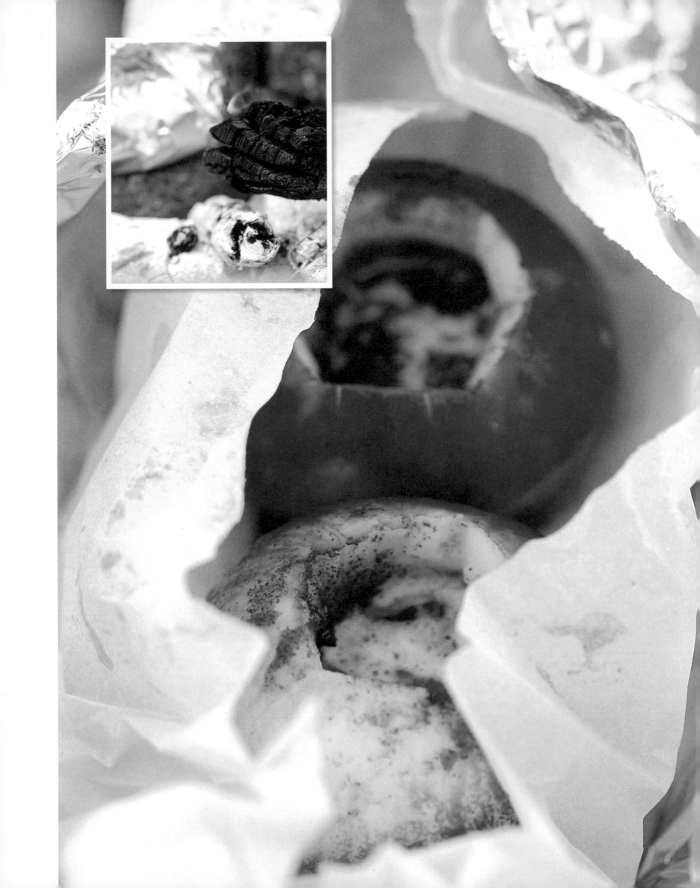

BARBECUED PEACHES

Actually, you can make these in the oven or the fire pit, as well as on the barbecue. Two of my favorite things are a peach pie with cardamom that I created, and a fruit crumble. This is an easy way to combine the two. This is perfect fire pit food for camping.

SERVES 6

3 peaches
3 tablespoons melted butter
½ cup (70 g) oats
½ cup (100 g) brown sugar
¼ cup (25 g) ground almonds
¼ teaspoon ground cardamom

1 Preheat the oven to 375°F/190°C/Gas 5 and line a 6–hole large muffin pan with paper baking cases.

2 Cut the peaches in half and remove the stone.

3 Put all the remaining ingredients in a bowl and mix together. Spoon the mixture evenly into each peach center. (Enlarge the dip with a spoon or melon ball scoop, if necessary.)

4 Place each peach half in a case, cover the whole thing with foil, and bake in the preheated oven for about one hour.

5 If you do this in the fire pit, wrap each peach in parchment (greaseproof) paper and then foil and place near the hot coals. Turn often. Peak inside. When the peaches are soft, melted, and gooey looking, they are ready to eat.

Variation: If you need to use peeled peaches because of a peach-skin phobia, then simply peel the peaches and slice them up. Drop about 5 slices of peach in each paper baking cup. Sprinkle the topping all over the top and push some in between the slices. Cover the whole pan with foil and bake as above.

SAVING PEACHES

I was going to do a lesson on canning peaches, but honestly, that is a rather intimidating procedure for anyone who has never canned food before. So, I am offering a very easy and fast way to preserve summer peaches. The freezer!

Ripe freestone peaches–as many or few as you feel like saving –they must be perfectly ripe (by this I mean not rock-hard or mushy soft; right in the middle of that.) Freestone simply means they come away from the pit (stone) easily.

1 Fill a large saucepan with water and set it over medium heat. Once it's really boiling, place about 3–4 peaches in the saucepan at a time. Don't pack the pan with peaches or they will just cook unevenly. You want to boil them for about 1–2 minutes, no more, gently moving them about with a spoon.

2 Remove the peaches with a slotted spoon and place them in big bowl of cold water in the sink. Run some cold water over them and make a small slit in the skin with a knife. The skin will just slip right off and you will have a naked peach.

3 Use your knife to cut the peach in half, then quarters, and then into 8 slices. They will come right off the pit (stone). Place the peach slices on a baking sheet. Continue until you have cooked, peeled ,and sliced all of your peaches.

4 Once the tray is filled, place it in the freezer. Leave the peaches to freeze solid and then remove them and drop into freezer bags. This way, they will not stick to each other and you can remove what you need, when you need it.

PISTOU

At first, I thought this was pesto spelt wrong. They are similar, but this doesn't have the nuts. It's good to have on hand for all sorts of summer foods. I use the mortar and pestle because it's good to do things by hand but also, to be honest, I personally enjoy pounding the heck out of something from time to time.

MAKES 1 SMALL JAR

A pinch of sea salt
1 garlic clove (or 2 if you love garlic!)
2 handfuls of fresh basil leaves
½ cup (40 g) finely grated Parmesan
A pinch of freshly ground black pepper
Olive oil

1 Sprinkle a bit of sea salt in the mortar, add the garlic, and pound them together with the pestle until the garlic becomes a paste.

2 Add some of the basil and crush it up with the pestle until it also becomes a paste. Continue adding more basil and pounding until it has all been used.

3 Begin to add the grated Parmesan. Add a drizzle of olive oil and blend well. Finish with pepper to taste. You should have a very green thick paste that tastes fabulous.

4 If you want to keep it in the fridge, decant to a bowl or jar, pour olive oil over top, and cover with plastic wrap (clingfilm) or a lid. It will keep for several days, but may darken on the top.

Serving suggestions: use pistou in pasta sauces, on bruschetta, in potato salad, on eggplant stacks, and in grilled sandwiches.

TIP: If you have plenty of fresh basil, make more pistou and freeze the extra in an ice-cube tray, pulling out a cube when needed for a pasta sauce.

OVEN-ROASTED TOMATOES

You can store these in the fridge to use over a week or so, but in my house they have never made it to the fridge —they simply get peeled off the tray, still warm, and eaten.

ABOUT 9 SLICES PER LARGE TOMATO

4 lovely ripe tomatoes of any size, thinly sliced
Sea salt
Freshly ground black pepper
Olive oil

1 Preheat the oven to 225°F/110°C/Gas ¼.

2 Line a baking tray with parchment (greaseproof) paper and lay the tomatoes on top.

3 Sprinkle on some sea salt and a pinch of black pepper. Drizzle with olive oil and bake in the preheated oven for about 2 hours and 20 minutes. They should look dry and should be crispy when you pick them up ... and pop them in your mouth.

SIMPLE SYRUP

This is a summer staple in my fridge. Simple Syrup is a must for all the summer classics—popsicles, ice teas, sorbets, snow cones, fruit salad, and the mojito. I make large batches as we like our sorbets ... and I like my mojitos. I use organic sugar, of course, so my syrup has a slight amber color. If you use regular sugar, it will be as clear as water.

MAKES 1½ CUPS

1 cup (200 g) granulated sugar
1 cup (240 ml) water

1 Combine the two ingredients in a saucepan and bring to a gentle boil over medium heat. Stir well until all the sugar has dissolved. Remove and let cool. Store in the fridge until needed.

FIVE-MINUTE EASY BLUEBERRY JAM

Again, I didn't want to scare you off with canning procedures and hot water baths, so this is an easy way to make jam for the family each week. You can use less sugar or more; it's up to you. These jams are stored in the fridge for about two weeks … if they last that long. Please use fresh lemons for your jam—I love the pulpy bits and real taste versus the bottled kind with sulfites.

MAKES 2 CUPS (480 ML)

3 cups (375 g) fresh blueberries
1 cup (200 g) granulated sugar
½ the juice from a fresh lemon (about ⅛ cup/30 ml)
¼ cup (60 ml) apple juice
¼ teaspoon ground cinnamon

1 Place all the ingredients in a large saucepan and bring to a boil, stirring often. Do not walk away from your saucepan as the level can rise fast and overspill.

2 Once the mix comes to a full rolling boil, turn the heat down to a gentle boil and cook for five minutes. You want bubbly action in the pan, not a simmer. Stir often.

3 After five minutes cooking, you will notice a bit of foam on top.Use a spoon to scrape and scoop this off and discard.

4 You can now decant into sterilized jars and store the jam in the fridge for about two weeks.

Variations: For Raspberry Jam, replace the blueberries with 3 cups (360 g) of raspberries and omit the apple juice and cinnamon. Follow the instructions above. Keep an eye during the boiling time, because raspberries have a terrible habit of sticking to the base of the pan. Makes 1½ cups (360 ml).

For strawberry jam, replace the blueberries with 1 lb (500 g) of hulled strawberries (left whole if small, quartered if large,) use ¼ cup (60 ml) lemon juice, and omit the apple juice and cinnamon. Follow the instructions above. You could also add a pinch of dried mint or some black pepper to the saucepan during cooking. Makes 2 cups.

TIP: I always use organic lemons—especially if I am using zest!

FALL

FOR BREAKFAST

Mini blueberry muffins
Pancake mix from scratch
Sunday scones
Scrambled ... well, everything
Zucchini (courgette) cakes with
    apple sauce

FOR DESSERT

Homemade marshmallows
Grandma's baked doughnuts
Bird's nest cookies
Baked apple pies
Caramel apples

FOR A MAIN MEAL

Tomato soup
Risotto
Mac and cheese
Chicken and kale soup
Chicken pot pie with puff pastry
Turkey chili
Yummy white baguettes
Homemade butter

FOR THE PANTRY

Salted caramel sauce
Apple sauce
Homemade vanilla extract

In Fall, we lock the gate, sit down, and watch the leaves turn fiery red.

LOVE ... Fall!

The farm is now closed. We can relax and fall back into routine. It's a comforting time of year, and so is the food. September is usually still very warm, but the nights are cold. The pantry and freezer are stocked up. We freeze blueberries, raspberries, and strawberries for smoothies, baking, or a straight-out-of-the-bag snack. We can tomatoes, peaches, and apple sauce as those are the favorites.

The apples are ready, so it's apple sauce time. The black beans are picked, dried, shelled, and stored. October is the time to plant the garlic. Fallen leaves are raked up and used as a mulch to protect the garlic over the winter and cover all the vegetable beds.

Herbs are gathered and dried either by hanging or using the dehydrator—dill, basil, rosemary, thyme, cilantro (coriander,) and bay leaves. I put them in canning jars and write the names with a felt marker. Lily can find the herbs we need either by reading the letters or recognizing the leaf. She's so proud when she finds the right one.

MINI BLUEBERRY MUFFINS

You can make these muffins large, if you prefer, using the same amount of mixture to fill a 12-hole muffin pan. I just feel more dainty eating small ones; plus mini is good for kids.

MAKES 24

1½ cups (200 g) all-purpose (plain) flour
¼ cup (150 g) granulated sugar
2 teaspoons baking powder
½ teaspoon salt
¼ cup (60 ml) vegetable oil
¼ cup (60 ml) Apple Sauce (see page 128)
1 egg
¼ cup (60 ml) milk
1 teaspoon vanilla extract
1 cup (125 g) fresh or frozen blueberries

FOR THE TOPPING:
2 teaspoons ground cinnamon
¼ cup (50 g) brown sugar

1 Preheat the oven to 375°F/190°C/Gas 5 and lightly butter a 24-hole mini-muffin pan, or use paper baking cups.

2 Put the flour, sugar, baking powder, and salt in a large bowl and combine. In a separate bowl, mix the oil, apple sauce, egg, milk, and vanilla.

3 Add the wet ingredients to the dry and then add the blueberries. Mix them in gently. Divide the mixture into the muffin cups.

4 To make the topping, mix the cinnamon and brown sugar together in a small bowl. Sprinkle over the tops of each muffin.

5 Bake the muffins in the preheated oven for 15 minutes.

PANCAKE MIX FROM SCRATCH

Nothing gets my girl moving like a pancake morning. She can set the table faster than I can crack an egg. We make a big batch of the dry mix to have on hand for weekends. I write the directions on the ziplock bag I keep it in so I don't have to dig around looking for the recipe.

MAKES ABOUT 4 BATCHES OF PANCAKES, EACH MAKING 6–8

FOR THE DRY MIX:
4 cups (565 g) all-purpose (plain) flour
1/8 cup (20 g) plus 2 teaspoons baking powder
2 teaspoons salt
Just under 1/2 cup (100 g) granulated sugar

FOR THE WET MIX:
1 1/8 cupS (275 ml) milk
1 egg
2 tablespoons melted butter

1 Mix all the dry ingredients together in a bowl and then transfer to a ziplock bag or airtight container and store away for pancake days.

2 When you are ready to make pancakes, simply blend together 1 cup (200 g) of the dry mix above with the wet ingredients. Blend well with a fork, but don't over-beat.

3 I like to wipe a wee bit of melted butter in the pan with a paper towel. Ladle in your pancakes—big, small, or sometimes I use a squeeze bottle to write words and make shapes. This brings big love my way.

SUNDAY SCONES

This is a basic recipe that you can add anything to: chopped chocolate pieces, candied ginger, orange or lemon zest, cinnamon, berries ... you'll notice I didn't say currants. I will never understand the currant—fresh or dried. I usually make one batch of scones and use three different fillings. Some with jam, some with fresh fruit, and some with cinnamon on top. Our favorite is all three at once!

MAKES ABOUT 8

¼ teaspoon salt

1 tablespoon baking soda (bicarbonate of soda)

¼ cup (40 g) baking powder

4 cups (565 g) all-purpose (plain) flour

¾ cup (160 g) cold unsalted butter

½ cup (100 g) granulated sugar, plus a little extra for brushing

1 cup (240 ml) heavy (double) cream, plus a little extra for brushing

¾ cup (180 ml) milk

1 teaspoon vanilla extract

FILLING AND TOPPING OPTIONS:

Sugar mixed with a little ground cinnamon, for sprinkling on top

Fresh or frozen fruit like peaches, blueberries, and raspberries

Jam-really good jam (use up the jams you made in the summer)

1 Preheat the oven to 400°F/200°C/Gas 6 and line a baking tray with parchment (greaseproof) paper.

2 Put the salt, baking soda (bicarbonate of soda), baking powder, and the flour in a bowl and mix together. Add the butter and use a pastry cutter to cut the butter and flour into each other until the butter resembles tiny peas. You can use your fingers to rub the ingredients together if you don'thave a cutter. Add the sugar and mix well.

3 Add the cream, milk, and vanilla to the flour and blend as best as you can with a fork or flat spoon.

4 Place the dough on a lightly floured surface. Gently knead for a few minutes until all the dried ingredients are blended in. Shape the dough into a rectangle and let rest, covered with a clean tea towel for 20 minutes.

5 Sprinkle a little flour on the work surface. Roll out the dough to about 2 in (5 cm) thick. Cut out your desired shapes—some like circles, some like squares, some prefer the triangle ... I'm a fan of random and rustic.

6 Once you have cut out your shapes, gently slice them in half. If you are using jam, you need to make a little indent—almost a pocket to hold the jam. Place about 1 tablespoon jam in the pocket, add some fresh fruit if you want, and then put the top lid back on and gently pinch the sides closed as best you can. If you are just adding some peach, berries, or apple slices, then you don't need to make a pocket or pinch the sides closed—just press the two closed like a sandwich.

7 Brush cream on the tops and sprinkle with sugar and cinnamon, or just sugar if preferred. Place the scones on the prepared sheet and bake in the preheated oven for 15 minutes if the scones are small or for 20 minutes if they are a bit larger. They should be golden brown when cooked.

SCRAMBLED ... WELL, EVERYTHING

Come fall time, it's about using up whatever is left in the garden. This is my idea of a very lazy lady omelette.

SERVES 2

3 slices of medium firm tofu

1 tablespoon butter

A few slices of diced onion, or chives

A big handful of spinach or kale

2 eggs (outside to the coop ... thank you ladies!)

A handful of cilantro (coriander,) a few sprigs of dill, and some thyme

A pinch of salt

½ cup (45 g) Cheddar cheese, grated

1 Chop the tofu into pieces and sauté in the butter until lightly brown.

2 Add the diced onion. Throw in your spinach or kale and cook until it begins to wilt.

3 Now add the eggs, chives (if using,) herbs, and a pinch of salt. Lastly, add your grated cheese. Let it melt for a minute and then enjoy.

ZUCCHINI (COURGETTE) CAKES WITH APPLE SAUCE

This is another attempt to use up the last of the zucchini (courgette). If the truth be told, we eat these year round. This is another recipe that you could play with—try wholewheat flour or add quinoa to the batter.

MAKES 4-6 CAKES

½ a zucchini (courgette), grated and patted dry in paper towel
¼ cup (30 g) minced shallot or leek (regular onion is fine to use)
A pinch of salt and freshly ground black pepper
½ cup (60 g) all-purpose (plain) flour
1 egg
1 cup (90 g) Cheddar cheese, grated
Butter or olive oil, for frying
Apple Sauce (see page 128), to serve

1 Blend all the ingredients in a bowl. Divide the mixture into portions and shape into patty shapes.

2 Fry the cakes over low to medium heat in a wee bit of butter or olive oil until very golden brown on each side. Flatten the cakes with your spatula to get them to cook through. They do not cook as fast as a pancake, so be patient and make sure they are cooked through.

3 Serve with your own homemade apple sauce.

TIP: Put the cakes on a cooling rack instead of on a plate after they are done; they build up moisture underneath and can become soggy while sitting.

TOMATO SOUP

If you were able to can up some tomatoes from the summer, this is the perfect recipe for them. Otherwise, buy the absolute best canned tomatoes you can find. Seriously, spend as much per can as you can afford to; it really does make a difference.

MAKES 16 CUPS

1 small onion, roughly chopped
¼ cup (60 g) butter
1 x 1¼ pint (796 ml) can of the best canned whole tomatoes you can find
    or a 1¾ pint (1 liter) size jar of your own tomatoes
A large handful of fresh basil
¾ cup (100 g) all-purpose (plain) flour
1 quart (1 liter) low-fat or whole milk
1 x 2¼ pint (1.36 liter) can tomato juice (you can buy a low-sodium version)
½ cup (100 g) granulated sugar
Salt and freshly ground black pepper

1 Sauté the onion in the butter in a large saucepan. Once the onion is soft, add the can of tomatoes and the basil. Cook for a few minutes until heated through. You can mash the tomatoes with a spoon.

2 Whisk the flour and milk together in a jug or bowl—don't worry about lumps, as it all gets whizzed up in the blender. Add the milk and flour to the saucepan. Cook until it thickens and then remove from the heat.

3 Transfer the soup to a food processor or blender and blitz until smooth—you may need to do this in batches. Blend until very, very smooth.

4 Pour it all back into the saucepan and add the can of tomato juice. Bring the soup back up to a good heat and stir in the sugar. Taste, and season with salt and pepper as you like.

RISOTTO

Most kids like white rice. Risotto works for kids because you can say it's fancy white rice. Topped off with some crème fraîche or Parmesan cheese ... yum. Another option would be to add some roasted wild mushrooms, but I've never met a kid super keen on a mushroom.

SERVES 4

6 cups (1.4 liters) vegetable stock
1 shallot, minced
2 garlic cloves, minced
Butter, for frying
A few sprigs of fresh thyme (or 1 teaspoon dried thyme)
2 cups (375 g) Arborio rice
1 small slice of Preserved Lemon (see page 153), minced superfine (or a few zests from a fresh lemon will do)
½ an apple, peeled and grated
1 baked butternut squash, peeled, deseeded, and chopped into chunks
Parmesan and crème fraîche, to serve, if you like

1 Heat your vegetable stock in a large saucepan.

2 In another large saucepan, sauté your minced shallot and garlic in some butter. Add the thyme, Arborio rice, preserved lemon, and the apple. Give it a few stirs to mix it well.

3 Keep the pan over a low to medium heat and add 1 cup (240 ml) of stock. Stir until it has been absorbed by the rice and then add another cup. Continue this until all your stock has been used. The rice should be thick and creamy—not solid nor super runny but a lovely nice place inbetween the two. Gently stir in the pre-baked squash chunks.

4 Now add your toppings of choice—freshly grated Parmesan or better yet, a big dollop of crème fraîche.

TIP: I throw the whole squash in the oven earlier in the day, or even the day before. Then it's all ready to go. Cut it in half and wrap in parchment and foil.

MAC AND CHEESE

This makes a large batch that I can freeze in containers for lunches or babysitters. For kids, I find keeping it simple is the best way. I like a fancy version with herbs, mustards, and exotic cheeses, but then I have to have it for lunch all week as no one else is eating it.

SERVES 8 KIDS OR 6 ADULTS

1 lb (500 g) macaroni noodles (or you can try spiral noodles ... always fun!)
½ cup (125 g) butter
½ cup (60 g) all-purpose (plain) flour
5 cups (1.2 liters) low-fat milk
3 cups (270 g) Cheddar cheese, grated
2 cups (180 g) Fontina cheese, grated
1 cup (90 g) Swiss cheese, grated
Salt

FOR THE TOPPING:
2 cups (85 g) Panko breadcrumbs
1 tablespoon butter

1 Preheat the oven to 350°F/180°C/Gas 4 and cook the macaroni noodles in a large saucepan of boiling salted water until done.

2 Melt the butter in a saucepan, add the flour, and whisk well. Add a splash of the milk and whisk until well blended. Slowly add more milk until it becomes smooth and lump free. Continue to add the rest of your milk stirring well. You can now add the three cheeses and stir until melted.

3 Spread the cooked macaroni in a 9 x 13 in (23 x 33 cm) casserole dish. Pour the cheese sauce over the top.

4 To make the topping, melt the butter in a frying pan. Add the Panko breadcrumbs and toast until lightly brown. Sprinkle the crisped breadcrumbs over the mac and cheese and bake in the preheated oven for about 20 minutes. It should be bubbly and heated through.

CHICKEN AND KALE SOUP

I can't tell you the joy I felt in my heart when my daughter declared that she loved this soup. It's so full of good healthy foods and is the perfect answer to the rainy day question: "What's for dinner?!" I like the mini pre-chopped bags of noodles for this soup, and red quinoa.

SERVES 5-6

1 small onion, finely chopped
2 tablespoons butter
10 cups (2.4 liters) vegetable stock
2 carrots, peeled and sliced
2 small bay leaves
½ teaspoon dried thyme (or 2 teaspoons fresh thyme leaves)
¾ cup (125 g) rice or 2 cups (250 g) noodles
¼ cup (45 g) quinoa
1 whole roasted chicken (either roast one the day before or buy one ready-roasted from the market)
½ a bunch of fresh kale (about 5 cups/200 g worth), roughly chopped
Salt and freshly ground black pepper

1 Sauté the onion in the butter until soft. Add the vegetable stock, carrots, bay leaves, thyme, rice or noodles, and the quinoa. Bring to a boil, reduce the heat, and simmer for about 25 minutes.

2 Add salt and pepper to taste and then the chopped kale. Simmer for a few minutes longer to cook the kale.

VARIATION: As an added bit of joy for this soup—grate some fresh parmesan cheese on top. Not the kind from a shaker, the block style!

CHICKEN POT PIE WITH PUFF PASTRY

Puff pastry is just plain fabulous. When we make this pot pie with puff pastry, everyone comes to the table. I use a whole roasted chicken for this recipe. You can either bake your own, or do what I do and buy one from the market that day.

MAKES TWO 8-IN (20-CM) PIES

2 leeks
¼ cup (60 g) butter
2 garlic cloves, minced
2 teaspoons freshly grated root ginger
1 teaspoon salt
1 teaspoon red curry paste (you may want more to spice it up)
1 teaspoon ground cumin

2–3 bay leaves, depending on size–mine are small so I use 3
1 x 14-oz (425-g) can of coconut milk
1 whole free-range roasted chicken, meat removed and chopped roughly
1 x 14-oz (425-g) can of cut green beans, drained
1 turnip, peeled, blanched, and cut up into small pieces
1 cup (40 g) freshly chopped cilantro (coriander)–if you loathe cilantro, leave it out; you could always add a handful of spinach, or kale, or swiss chard, instead
1 package of puff pastry, thawed

1 Preheat the oven to 400°F/200°C/Gas 6.

2 Slice up your leeks using all the whites and just the beginning part of the green. Sauté the leeks in the butter in a large saucepan until soft. Add your minced garlic and cook for a few minutes.

3 Add the ginger, salt, curry paste, cumin, and bay leaves. Cook for a few more minutes together to distribute the curry paste evenly. Now add your coconut milk and let it come to a good simmer for few minutes.

4 Add the chicken, turnip, and cilantro (coriander.) Mix together well and then remove from the heat.

5 Divide the filling between two pie plates. Roll out the puff pastry on a lightly floured surface and use it to cover each pie.

6 Bake in the preheated oven for 25 minutes until the pastry is golden brown.

NOTE: This recipe was a complete accident. I'm terribly dyslexic and I misread ... well, pretty much everything. It worked out in the end, though, as I created this dish!

TURKEY CHILI

This is perfect for curling up with on a cold fall night. Lily and I set up a line of toppings for our chili that includes cheeses, taco chips, cilantro (coriander,) bacon, quinoa, and sour cream. We have to steal one of Daddy's beers for this recipe, too, which always gets us in trouble.

MAKES 8 BOWLS

1 sweet onion, finely chopped

2 garlic cloves, crushed

2 tablespoons butter

2 lb (1 kg) ground (minced) turkey

2 teaspoons salt

1 bottle of beer (a dark ale is best)

1 x 14-oz (400-g) can of really good crushed tomatoes

1 x 14-oz (400-g) can of cannellini beans, drained

1 cup (240 g) pinto beans

3 tablespoons chili powder

1 teaspoon curry powder

¼ teaspoon ground ginger

½ cup (140 g) runny honey

1 x 4.5-oz (135-g) can of chopped green chili (if you like it hotter, you could use a small fresh green chili)

1 Sauté the onion and garlic in the butter in a large saucepan until soft but not brown.

2 Brown the turkey in a separate saucepan until all the pink has gone. Drain off the excess fat and add the meat to the onion.

3 Add the remaining ingredients to the large saucepan, giving a good stir. Bring to a boil and stir well. Reduce the heat and let simmer for about 30 minutes, stirring often.

4 Serve with a variety of toppings in separate bowls for all to add as they please—grated cheeses, chopped green onions (spring onions,) nacho chips, sour cream, bacon, cilantro (coriander,) and yes, I like to add quinoa whenever I can!

YUMMY WHITE BAGUETTES

There are four ingredients in these baguettes, but they taste just lovely. When they are warm and straight out of the oven ... wow. Seriously ... wow!

MAKES 4

4 cups (565 g) white bread flour
1 teaspoon salt
1 ⅔ cups (400 ml) warm water (but you may need
  an extra 2 tablespoons if the dough seems too dry)
2 teaspoons traditional dried yeast

1 To make the dough, follow the instructions on page 34.

2 Divide the dough in half and then in quarters. You want four equal pieces of dough. Take each piece and fold the outsides over into the center. Bring all sides over and using your fingertips, press them into the center of each piece. You should work toward forming a longer baguette style piece of dough.

3 Place the baguettes on a baking tray lined with parchment (greaseproof) paper. You may need to use two trays as all four pieces may not fit on one. Cover with the cloth again and let rise for another hour.

4 Time to bake! Preheat the oven to 450°F/230°C/ Gas 8. Bake two loaves at a time, if you can't fit four in your oven. Bake in the preheated oven for 10 minutes or so until the loaves are a rich golden brown. Too light a brown in color, and they may not be cooked inside. Tap the bottom of the tin and if it sounds hollow, the bread should be baked.

HOMEMADE BUTTER

If you are going to make homemade bread, then go one step further and make the butter—even just once so you can impress your friends or show your kids how it's done.

MAKES ABOUT ¾ CUP

2 cups (480 ml) whipping cream
⅛ teaspoon Himalayan sea salt (optional)

1 Put the cream in an electric stand mixer and set it to medium speed to begin with. Once it starts to thicken, you can increase the speed. You may need to stop the machine and scrape the sides down a few times. The cream will start to thicken and then will eventually begin to separate. It should take about 14 minutes.

2 You will see a liquid separating from the butter lumps. This is buttermilk and you can save it for making waffles or pancakes.

3 Pour off the buttermilk and drop the lumps into a few layers of cheesecloth (muslin.) Squeeze it gently and knead it under running cold water. You want to get all the buttermilk out.

4 You can eat this butter as it is, or add some sea salt. Make an indent to pour the salt into, then gently knead the butter so the salt is worked through the butter. You could also knead in fresh herbs, sun-dried tomatoes,or garlic. The butter can be kept in the fridge for five days.

TIP: Don't walk away or mentally fade off in a daydream when making butter. Once the separation happens, the liquid will fly out of the bowl all over your kitchen. This is what I've been told ... it's not like I did it twice in a row or anything!

HOMEMADE MARSHMALLOWS

If you haven't made marshmallows before, then you MUST! They are easy, fun, and will make the packaged marshmallows blush in shame. You can add natural flavors or coatings to these, like strawberry or coconut, or you can dip them in chocolate, but here in Canada, it's all about the s'more—a toasted marshmallow, a graham cracker (digestive biscuit), and a chunk of chocolate. To solve the problem of getting the chocolate to melt between the marshmallow and cracker, I pre-melt some chocolate and spread it on the cracker ahead. Brilliant! Thank You.

MAKES ABOUT 48

3 packages of gelatin–¼ oz (5 g) each package
 or ¾ oz (21 g) in total
1 cup (240 ml) cold water
2 cups (200 g) granulated sugar
⅔ cup (200 g) light corn syrup (liquid glucose)
¼ teaspoon salt
2 teaspoons vanilla extract
2 cups (275 g) icing sugar, for coating the marshmallows

1 Put the three packages of gelatin and ½ cup (120 ml) of the cold water in an electric stand mixer. Let rest for about 15 minutes.

2 Combine the sugar, remaining water, corn syrup, and salt in a saucepan and bring to a boil, stirring constantly. Once a full boil is reached, reduce the heat a pinch, and boil for two minutes. Pour the hot mix into your mixer over the gelatin. Beat on a high speed for 10 minutes—it will become very thick toward the end. Once it's super-thick, add your vanilla and beat for another minute.

3 While the marshmallows are beating, line a 9 x 13 in (12 x 33 cm) casserole dish with plastic wrap (clingfilm)—sides too. Take some vegetable oil and rub it all over the plastic wrap (cling film) in the casserole dish—sides too! Now rub the oil on your spatula and a pair of kitchen scissors or a knife. Once the marshmallow is ready, rub the oil on your hands too.

4 Scrape out the marshmallow into the dish. Use your spatula to get it out and spread it as even as you can in the dish. Let sit for 2–3 hours. It will firm up into one solid piece.

5 After it has set, use your oil-coated knife or scissors to cut strips and then pieces—you can make them large or small. Take each piece and dip all sides in icing sugar. This will keep them from sticking to each other and anything they come in contact with.

6 They are now ready for a cup of Homemade Cocoa (see page 69), campfire roast, or the best-ever rice crispy squares!

GRANDMA'S BAKED DOUGHNUTS

My husband's mom made these for him as an after-school treat, 40 years ago! Now, I make them as an after-school treat for my girl. This is the kind of treat that your kids' friends will love you for ... they must be served warm from the oven. There really is no other way.

MAKES 24

¼ cup (60 g) softened butter
6 tablespoons granulated sugar
1 egg
½ teaspoon vanilla extract
⅓ cup (80 ml) milk
⅓ teaspoon salt
¼ teaspoon nutmeg
1 ¼ cup (170 g) all-purpose (plain) flour
2 teaspoons baking powder

FOR THE COATING:

½ cup (50 g) granulated sugar
1 ½ tablespoons ground cinnamon
½ cup (115 g) melted butter

1 Preheat the oven to 350°F/180°C/Gas 4 and grease two 12-hole mini-muffin pans.

2 Beat the butter with the sugar in a bowl. Add the egg, vanilla, and milk and mix together.

3 Mix the salt, nutmeg, flour, and baking powder together in another bowl. Slowly add the dry mix to the wet. Blend well and then spoon the mixture into the greased mini-muffin pan. Fill each hole halfway. Bake in the preheated oven for 10–12 minutes.

4 While the doughnuts are baking, make the coating. Mix the sugar and cinnamon in a bowl and put the melted butter in a separate bowl.

5 Once the doughnuts are removed from the oven, dip them in the butter, and then roll them in the sugar and cinnamon mixture. Eat them now!

BIRD'S NEST COOKIES

These cookies always remind me of my grandma—not that she ever made them. Her idea of cooking was frying spam in brown sugar. she just bought the packaged version. These cookies are all about the jam in the center, so it must be the best jam you can get your hands on.

MAKES ABOUT 25

2 cups (260 g) all-purpose (plain) flour
½ teaspoon salt
½ teaspoon baking powder
1 cup (225 g) unsalted butter, softened
½ cup (50 g) granulated sugar
1 egg yolk
1½ teaspoons almond extract
1 cup (80 g) sliced almonds, roughly crushed with your hands
1 jar of the best jam you can find (we use Missing Goat Raspberry Jam)

1 Preheat the oven to 350°F/180°C/Gas 4 and line a baking sheet with parchment (greaseproof) paper.

2 Mix the flour, salt, and baking powder together in a bowl. Blend the butter and sugar in another bowl and add the egg yolk and almond extract. Add the flour mixture to your butter bowl and blend well.

3 Form golf-ball size dough balls and roll them in the almonds. Press the nuts in gently if needed. Place the coated balls on the baking sheet. Press holes in the center of each ball for the jam —BUT DO NOT add the jam yet—I make the holes extra large!

4 Bake the dough balls in the preheated oven for five minutes and then remove from the oven. Now, you can add the jam—as much as you can fit in the hole—about 1 heaped tablespoon.

5 Put them back in the oven for 12–14 minutes until just slightly brown.

BAKED APPLE PIES

I've struggled with apple pie for years. The filling was never right. The apples were never cooked, or I would overcook the dough trying to cook the apples inside ... grrr. Now I have it! As cute as these are in little canning jars, this recipe can also be made into a regular sized pie ... the choice is yours! This way is guaranteed to get you some extra oohs and ahhs, though!

MAKES ABOUT 8 CANNING JAR (4 FL OZ/125 ML) PIES
or you can make one large pie in a Pyrex dish (see Variation opposite)

1 batch of pie dough (pastry) (see page 48)

FOR THE FILLING:
6 apples, peeled and sliced thin (I use Gala apples)
½ cup (120 ml) apple juice
¾ cup (75 g) granulated sugar–this really depends on your apple and whether it's sweet or tart–taste and adjust the amount of sugar as needed
¼ teaspoon salt
1 teaspoon ground cinnamon
¼ teaspoon ground cloves
A pinch of ground nutmeg
⅛ cup (30 g) unsalted butter
3 tablespoons all-purpose (plain) flour
Cream and sugar, for sprinkling on tops

1 Preheat the oven to 425°F/220°C/Gas 7.

2 If you are using the small canning jars, you will need to cut the apple slices in half so that they fit in the jar. If you are making a pie, just leave them in long thin slices. Place the apple pieces and apple juice in a saucepan, bring to a boil, and simmer gently, stirring often, for 10 minutes.

3 Add the sugar, salt, spices, and butter and stir well. Add the flour and stir really well—it will thicken nicely.

4 Spoon the filling into the canning jars—you should be able to fill about 8 jars. They should be three-quarters full.

5 Make the pastry using the method on page 48 but roll out to about ¼ in (3 mm). Peel off the top layer of wax paper and sprinkle on a bit of flour. Flip the dough over onto the work surface. Add a little flour there, too, and peel off the other sheet of wax paper. If it seems sticky, sprinkle a wee bit of flour over the dough. Now use the canning jar you are going to be baking in to cut out circles for gthe lids. Place your circle of pie dough on top of each jar and press down the edges. Brush the dough with cream and sprinkle with sugar. Place the jars on a baking sheet to bake.

6 Bake in the preheated oven for 10 minutes and then turn the heat down to 350°F/180°C/Gas 4 for another 15 minutes.

VARIATION: If you would prefer to make one large pie, roll out your dough for a top and bottom to line an 8-in (20-cm) pie plate. Lay your bottom layer of dough in the pie plate. Pour the filling in and then add your dough top. Cut a few slits in the top for steam to escape, brush the top of the pie with cream, and sprinkle with sugar. Bake in an oven preheated to 425°F/220°C/Gas 7 for 10 minutes and then reduce the temperature to 350°F/180°C/Gas 4 for another 25 minutes.

CARAMEL APPLES

I've never liked eating a plain apple. But, cover it in caramel, then call my name! I took one basic recipe, and discovered two treats that can be made from it. A candy thermometer is needed for this.

MAKES 6

1 cup (240 ml) heavy (double) cream
1 cup (100 g) granulated sugar
¾ cup (250 g) corn syrup (golden syrup)
½ cup (115 g) butter
1 teaspoon vanilla extract
6 sticks from the garden or you can use chop sticks
6 apples of your choice, washed

OPTIONAL TOPPINGS: Crushed nuts • Smarties • Mini marshmallows • Melted chocolate

1 Put the cream, sugar, and corn syrup (golden syrup) in a large saucepan and bring to a boil. Reduce the heat, but keep the mixture boiling—you want to bring it to a temperature of 245°F/118°C. Remove the saucepan from the heat and let settle for a minute or two. Add the butter and vanilla and stir well.

2 Push the sticks into the washed apples. Swirl them one by one in the caramel mixture. If you are using nuts or other toppings, then dip them now. Let cool on a sheet of parchment (greaseproof) paper. Once cool, you can drizzle with melted chocolate if you like.

CARAMEL CHEWS: If you have caramel left over, drizzle it (about 1½ cups) on a sheet of parchment (greaseproof) paper. Melt half a cup of chocolate and pour this over the caramel. Sprinkle on some chopped nuts of your choice (pistachios are delicious.) Let cool and set and then cut into chunks.

SALTED CARAMEL SAUCE

Take the caramel, and then add salt ... this, to me, is heaven—on ice cream, over cake, or for dipping apples into. My favorite way to eat this ... on a spoon. Repeat, repeat, repeat.

MAKES 1 CUP (200 ML) SAUCE

½ cup (115 g) unsalted butter
¼ cup (50 g) brown sugar
¼ cup (50 g) granulated sugar
¼ cup (85 g) corn syrup (golden syrup)
½ cup (120 ml) heavy (double) cream
¼ teaspoon really good-quality salt (I have pink Himalayan
    sea salt ... I just like to say that; it sounds fancy)

1 Put all the ingredients in a saucepan. Stir together and bring to a boil. Reduce the heat to a nice gentle boil for about five minutes, and then it's done.

2 Let cool a bit or you will burn your tongue. (This is what I've heard. I'm not a savage who dives into hot caramel sauce right off the stove. Ok, I am.)

3 Serve it warm on anything. Or you can keep it in a jar in the fridge to use when needed. It will thicken right up in the fridge, but a few seconds in the microwave and it's pourable again.

APPLE SAUCE

Possibly the simplest thing to preserve for the year. We double or even triple this recipe and freeze it in little ziplock bags—about 1 cup (290 g) per bag. We make all different types of apple sauce—unsweetened, sweetened, cinnamon, blueberry apple sauce (we call it Blause,) and a spiced, holiday version with cloves.

MAKES ABOUT 3 CUPS (870 G) SAUCE

5 apples (we use our own apples, but we don't know the variety–they are a sweeter apple, much like a Gala)
1 cup (240 ml) apple juice
¼ cup (50 g) granulated sugar (you can leave it out if your apple is sweet or add more if you like–if you keep it simple, it can be sweetened later depending what your use is)
½ teaspoon ground cinnamon (optional)

1 Peel and core the apples. Chop them up and place in a large saucepan.

2 Add the apple juice, bring to a boil, and then reduce the heat slightly to a very gentle boil.

3 Cook for about 20 minutes. Now add your sugar and spices if you are using them. You just made apple sauce.

HOMEMADE VANILLA EXTRACT

I haven't bought vanilla extract in years. It's so easy and I just keep topping it up when it runs low. This makes a fun gift for the holidays, and now is the perfect time to make it as it's good to leave it to sit for a few months.

MAKES 1 JAR

3–4 vanilla beans (pods) per jar
Vodka

1 Split open the vanilla beans (pods) and drop them in a jar with a lid (I use a canning jar.)

2 Pour vodka over and fill to the top. Fasten the lid and give a shake. Done. Wasn't that ridiculously easy?

3 Give it a good shake every few days. After 6–8 weeks it will really darken in color and be a very rich vanilla extract to use in baking. When it starts to run low, just top it off with more vodka. You can add another split bean (pod) too.

NOTE: You can make this in any size jar you like. The one I am showing you is 1½ cups, but the choice is yours. If you use a larger jar, just add a few more beans.

WINTER

FOR BREAKFAST

Baked French toast or Bread Pudding
Breakfast to go
Kitchen sink muffins

FOR A MAIN MEAL

Baked beans with salsa
Lasagna made with fresh pasta
Perogies (or pierogi)
Chicken strips
Eggplant (aubergine) Parmesan

FOR DESSERT

Gingerbread cookies
Macaroons
Rice pudding with cardamom
Mini jam pies

FOR THE PANTRY

Fruit and seed crackers
Preserved Meyer lemons
Blueberry syrup
Dog biscuits
Garlic mash for chickens

Everything is asleep in the garden;
our snowy world is silent.

LOVE ... Winter!

Our winters here in Vancouver, British Columbia, are very wet and frosty cold. We have small snowfalls, but now and then, we get a winter wonderland. On a blustery wet day, what could be better than some good old-fashioned oatmeal with ground flax seeds, mashed banana, and garlic! Don't worry, I'm talking about a garlic mash for chickens. The hens love it—garlic is great for their health and immune system, and it warms them up from the inside out.

For Oliver, our dog, we have homemade dog biscuits. He loves them but let's be honest, he'll eat just about anything, including gum boots. He' not fussy, but I know what's in them, and it makes Lily happy to bake him something special, which is what it's all about.

You can now give away your homemade vanilla for the holidays, and start your preserved lemons for using throughout the year. Make some jars for a friend too. They are pretty and delicious.

BAKED FRENCH TOAST OR BREAD PUDDING

You already know we love French toast, so of course, here is another version. But here is the beauty of this recipe: it can also be bread pudding with rum sauce. It's breakfast or dessert or, in my case, both. This recipe can be made the day before and baked in the morning, or you can make it in the morning and bake it while you eat dinner.

SERVES 6 (WITH A BIT TO SPARE FOR SECONDS)

1 tablespoon butter
1 loaf of bread
8 eggs
4 cups (1½ pints) milk
1 cup (240 ml) heavy (double) cream
1 cup (200 g) granulated sugar
¼ teaspoon cloves
1 teaspoon ground cinnamon
1 tablespoon vanilla paste or
    2 teaspoons vanilla extract
¼ teaspoon salt

FOR THE RUM SAUCE (OPTIONAL):

2 tablespoons butter
1 tablespoon cornstarch (cornflour)
½ cup (125 ml) milk
½ cup (125 ml) heavy (double) cream
⅛ teaspoon salt
½ cup (100 g) granulated sugar
⅛–¼ cup (30–60 ml) rum (depends how much
    you like rum!)

1 Preheat the oven to 350°F/180°C/Gas 4 and butter a 9 x 13 in (23 x 33 cm) casserole dish.

2 Tear your loaf of bread into chunks and drop them in the prepared dish. In another bowl, add your eggs, milk, cream, sugar, spices, vanilla, and salt. Beat together well and then pour the mixture over the bread.

3 If you are baking this the next day, or later in the day, then cover it with plastic wrap (clingfilm) and place it in the fridge. You will need to let it sit for at least one hour before baking so the bread can soak up the liquid.

4 Bake in the preheated oven for 40–45 minutes until golden on top. Serve with maple syrup and fruit or with Blueberry Syrup (see page 154) for breakfast.

5 Alternatively, make this rum sauce to serve with the bread pudding as a dessert. Melt the butter in a saucepan and whisk in the cornstarch (cornflour.) Add the milk, cream, salt, and sugar. Whisk well and stir until it begins to thicken a bit. Add the rum and stir to mix. Serve warm, poured over the bread pudding.

BREAKFAST TO GO

This is what I like to call a "road-trip breakfast." It's your average breakfast disguised as a muffin to go.

MAKES 6

2 slices of bread, cut into cubes
6 cooked bacon rashers, broken into pieces (these can be prepared the day before, but make sure they are crispy!)
1 cup (90 g) Cheddar cheese, grated
4 eggs
¼ cup (60 ml) milk or cream

1 Preheat the oven to 350°F/180°C/Gas 4 and line a 6-hole muffin pan with paper baking cups.

2 Put the bread cubes in a bowl and add the bacon pieces. Throw in your cheese and give a good toss so it's all mixed together. Spoon the mix into the muffin cups, filling each one.

3 Mix the eggs and milk or cream together in a bowl and pour this over the bread mixture in each muffin cup. You can sprinkle a bit more cheese on the tops if liked.

4 Bake in the preheated oven for about 15 minutes until you see the egg is firmly set. Hit the road.

VARIATIONS: Add a splash of hot sauce or some sautéed onions to the top of each muffin before baking to ring the changes.

KITCHEN SINK MUFFINS

This is a really useful recipe. It's the kind of muffin that you can throw just about anything in—nuts, raisins, berries, pumpkin seeds, dried fruits, chocolate chips, pineapple .... It's the whatever-you-have-around-the-kitchen muffin.

MAKES ABOUT 18

2½ cups (340 g) all-purpose (plain) flour
1 cup (200 g) granulated sugar
1 teaspoon baking powder
½ teaspoon salt
2 teaspoons baking soda (bicarbonate of soda)
¼ cup (40 ml) coconut oil
¾ cup (125 ml) vegetable oil
3 eggs
1 banana, mashed
1 cup (240 g) apple sauce (shop-bought
     or see page 128 if you want to make your own)
2 teaspoons vanilla extract
1 cup (135 g) grated carrot
1 cup (160 g) chocolate chips
1 cup (125 g) fresh or frozen raspberries
½ cup (70 g) dates, chopped

1 Preheat the oven to 350°F/180°C/Gas 4 and line about 18 holes in one or two muffin pans with paper baking cups.

2 Put the flour, sugar, baking powder, salt, and baking soda (bicarbonate of soda) in a bowl and mix well.

3 Put the coconut oil, vegetable oil, eggs, mashed banana, apple sauce, and vanilla in another bowl and mix well. Mix the wet and dry ingredients together.

4 Add the grated carrot, chocolate chips, raspberries, and chopped dates. Mix gently so the berries don't go to mush.

5 Fill each paper baking cup to the top and then bake in the preheated oven for about 25 minutes—do a toothpick check: if it comes out clean, they are done. If not, bake for another 5–10 minutes.

BAKED BEANS WITH SALSA

My girl loves her baked beans in a bowl with toast. My sister-in-law would put them over lentils for her kids, and I prefer them in a freshly made warm tortilla with salsa. Or on my hot dog (did I just type that?) This is another good dish to freeze for those crazy busy days when you don't want to cook.

SERVES 6
(more if you are using in wraps as a burrito)

1 small shallot
1 garlic clove
1 x 14-oz (400-g) can chopped or whole tomatoes
1 teaspoon salt
¼ cup (50 g) brown sugar
¼ cup (70 g) molasses (treacle)
7-8 cooked bacon rashers, chopped
3 x 14-oz (400-g) cans cooked beans (white beans, cannelloni beans, and navy beans,) drained
3 tablespoons butter
1 batch of tortillas (see page 62), to serve

FOR THE SALSA:
(I also use this salsa for nachos, burritos, and quesadillas)
1 avocado, chopped
1/2 a sweet red onion, finely chopped
2 fresh tomatoes, chopped
Juice of 1 lime (and a pinch of lime zest is nice)
A handful of freshly chopped cilantro (coriander)
A pinch of salt
1-2 fresh green chilies, deseeded and finely chopped (optional)

1 Preheat the oven to 350°F/180°C/Gas 4.

2 Put the shallot, garlic, and tomatoes in a food processor or blender. Blitz them together until they are a smooth sauce. Add the salt, brown sugar, and molasses (treacle) and blitz again.

3 Put the chopped bacon rashers and drained beans in a large casserole dish and toss them together so they are all mixed up. Pour the sauce over the beans and stir together. Place three dollops of butter on top, cover with foil, and bake in the preheated oven for 40 minutes. Remove the foil, give it a stir, and then bake for another 15 minutes.

4 While they are cooking, make the salsa. Toss all the ingredients together in a bowl and refrigerate until ready to use. It won't keep very well overnight, because the avocado browns, so is best eaten on the same day.

5 Serve the beans in warm tortillas with a dollop of fresh salsa.

LASAGNA MADE WITH FRESH PASTA

I never really liked lasagna. It was ok, and my sister-in-law Kelly and her husband make a fabulous one. But I always hated the crispy edges of the pasta that never cooked. It was always a little disappointing. Then I made fresh pasta. Wow—huge difference and so good.

SERVES 6

1 batch of Pasta from Scratch (see page 41)
Vegetable oil, for frying
1 small onion
4 carrots, sliced
2 cups (200 g) mozzarella cheese, grated
2 cups (450 g) ricotta cheese
A handful of fresh basil or 1-2 tablespoons of dried basil
2 eggs
1 x 23-fl oz (700-ml) jar of your favorite tomato/pasta sauce
1 bunch of kale, finely chopped
1 cup (80 g) Parmesan cheese, freshly grated

1 Preheat the oven to 350°F/180°C/Gas 4.

2 Make the pasta following the instructions on page 41. The joy of making lasagna is you just need thin sheets. The extra dough can be made into spaghetti or wide noodles and kept in the fridge for another day. You will need about nine strips of fresh pasta—nice and thin.

3 Heat a little oil in a frying pan and sauté the onion over medium heat until softened. Cook the carrots in a saucepan of boiling water until softened.

4 Mix the mozzarella, ricotta, basil, eggs, and the cooked onion together in a bowl. Keep the cooked carrots and kale to the side for layering.

5 Place a few tablespoons of the pasta sauce on the bottom of a 9 x 13 in (23 x 33 cm) baking dish.

6 Lay down your first set of pasta strips to cover the bottom of the dish—they can overlap a wee bit if needed to make them fit, or you can trim them to fit. Spread half of the cheese mixture over the pasta and sprinkle with the kale. Lay down more pasta to cover the kale. Spread over the remaining cheese mixture and then top with the cooked carrots. Top this with the last layer of pasta.

7 Pour the rest of the pasta sauce all over the pasta right to the edge of the dish. Sprinkle with the Parmesan cheese and then bake in the preheated oven for 45 minutes until golden on top.

PEROGIES (OR PIEROGI)

This is a good recipe to make with your friends and a bottle of wine. My girl is pretty good at pinching them closed, too. Perogies are a Polish dish and are like a sort of savory dumpling. To get the dough thin enough you really need a pasta maker. It rolls the dough out so thin and lovely.

MAKES ABOUT 70 SMALL PEROGIES OR 35 LARGER ONES

FOR THE DOUGH:
4 cups (565 g) strong bread flour
2 eggs
½ cup (125 ml) sour cream
1 teaspoon salt
⅔ cup (160 ml) warm water

FOR THE POTATO AND CHEESE FILLING:
1 russet potato, boiled or baked
1 tablespoon butter
½ cup (45 g) Cheddar cheese, grated
¼ cup (55 g) ricotta
2 tablespoons fresh dill or 1 tablespoon dried dill
2 tablespoons snipped chives or scallions (spring onions)
A pinch of salt and freshly ground black pepper

FOR THE YAM, GOAT'S CHEESE, AND CARAMELIZED ONION FILLING:
1 yam
1 sweet onion, thinly sliced
2 tablespoons butter
¼ cup (50 g) goat's cheese

1 Put all the dough ingredients in a bowl and mix well. Turn the dough out onto a lightly floured surface and knead until you have a well-blended and smooth dough.

2 Get your pasta maker out. I cut the dough into three pieces and start working one at a time through the machine (you will need to cut the dough as it gets long.) You should end up with long strips. Lay these out on the floured surface and cut out circles—I use a canning jar to cut my perogie circles, but you can make them large or small.

3 Pull any dough together that is left over after cutting out circles, knead, and then work it through the machine again. Be sure to flour your work surface well so the dough doesn't stick. It can tear easily and then is no good.

4 Sprinkle some flour on a baking sheet lined with parchment (greaseproof) paper. Lay the cut out circles on the lined sheet and cover with plastic wrap (clingfilm) while you make the rest.

5 To make the potato filling: Peel and mash the cooked potato with the butter. Add the two types of cheese, dill, and salt and pepper and mix well. Spoon about 1½ teaspoons of the filling into the center of each circle. Fold the dough over to make a semi-circle and pinch the edges closed really well. Be sure to keep your work surface well floured as you work.

6 To make the yam filling: Wrap the yam in parchment (greaseproof) paper and then in foil. Bake it in an oven preheated to 375°F/190°C/Gas 5 for one hour. You can do this the day before. When the yam is cooked, remove the peel and mash the yam in a bowl. Caramelize the onion in a frying pan with a little butter until browned and delicious. Add to the mashed yam

along with the goat's cheese and mix well. Spoon about 1½ teaspoons of the filling into the center of each circle. Fold the dough over to make a semi-circle and pinch the edges closed really well. Be sure to keep your work surface well floured as you work.

7 Bring a large saucepan of salted water to a boil. Drop the perogies in—about 10 at a time if they are small, 6 at a time if large. Once they float to the top, they are ready to scoop out. This should take about five minutes.

To serve (optional): Sprinkle with extra cheese, fried onions, or bacon and dip in sour cream. Sauerkraut is also enjoyed by some with these. By some I said!

CHICKEN STRIPS

I can't buy chicken strips from the store. They have so many ingredients I don't recognize, or way too much salt. Plus, they really are easy to make at home anyway.

SERVES 2-3

2 boneless chicken breasts
1 egg, beaten
½ cup (50 g) roughly ground almonds
½ cup (20 g) Panko breadcrumbs (any breadcrumbs, fresh or dried, will work)
A pinch of salt
Olive oil or vegetable oil, for drizzling.

1 Preheat the oven to 350°F/180°C/Gas 4 and line a baking sheet with parchment (greaseproof) paper.

2 Cut your chicken breasts into strips. (I have learnt from a friend to use scissors for cutting meat. Brilliant. You probably knew this, but I did not!)

3 Place the beaten egg in a shallow bowl. Place the almonds, breadcrumbs, and salt in another shallow bowl next to it and mix together.

4 Dip each chicken strip in the egg and then roll it in the breadcrumb mixture. Place the coated strips on the prepared sheet.

5 Once all your strips are coated and on the baking sheet, drizzle a wee bit of oil over each one. Bake in the preheated oven for 12 minutes, turn over, and then bake for another 12 minutes until golden and crisp all over.

NO-NAME DIP: The kids go for the ketchup right away, but I love to eat mine with this very silly dip:

Put ¼ cup (50 g) mayonnaise, ½ cup (50 g) sour cream, and 1 heaped tablespoon of Dijon mustard in a bowl. Mix well and serve with your chicken strips.

Now, about this picture. I'm sorry, but I had a whole tray full when I went to get the camera. I'm lucky to have found this one lonely strip left to photograph. I felt sorry for him for being left alone ... it passed ... I ate him.

EGGPLANT (AUBERGINE) PARMESAN

My husband and I like this. My girl doesn't—she can't always win.
I bake the eggplant (aubergine) instead of frying it because it's
much easier, cleaner, and slightly better health-wise.

SERVES 4

2–3 eggs, beaten

2–3 cups (100–150 g) breadcrumbs or Panko
   breadcrumbs

1 large eggplant (aubergine), sliced into thin
   circles

Vegetable oil, for drizzling

1 onion, finely chopped

3 garlic cloves, crushed

1 x 23-fl oz (700-ml) jar of your favorite tomato
   or pasta sauce

4 tomatoes, thinly sliced

1 large block of mozzarella, thinly sliced

1 cup (80 g) Parmesan cheese, grated

1 Preheat the oven to 350°F/180°C/Gas 4 and line a
baking sheet with parchment (greaseproof) paper.

2 Put the beaten eggs in a shallow bowl. Place the
breadcrumbs in another shallow bowl. Dip the eggplant
(aubergine) slices in the egg and then the breadcrumbs.
Lay the coated slices on the prepared baking sheet.

3 When all the eggplant (aubergine) is on the lined tray,
drizzle each slice with vegetable oil, and then bake in the
preheated oven for about 20 minutes. Flip each piece
and bake for another 20 minutes until the slices are crispy
and golden.

4 Heat a little oil in a frying pan and sauté the onion and garlic
together over medium heat until soft and lightly browned.

5 Pour some of the tomato sauce over the base of a
9 x 13 in (23 x 33 cm) casserole dish. Place your first
eggplant (aubergine) circles on the bottom—you may fit 6–8
circles, it depends on the size of your eggplant. You are
going to make tall layers or towers of eggplant (aubergine.)

6 Once you have the base of the dish covered, sprinkle a
bit of your cooked onion on each circle. Divide it equally
between the 6–8 circles. Lay down a slice of tomato and
then a slice of mozzarella cheese on top of the onion. Top
with another eggplant (aubergine) circle and then more
tomato and mozzarella. Repeat these layers again, ending
with a slice of mozzarella

7 Pour the jar of sauce over all the towers, sprinkle with the
Parmesan cheese, and bake in the preheated oven for
about 40 minutes.

GINGERBREAD COOKIES

We make these every year and hang them on our kitchen cookie tree. It's one of those projects that I love and wait for all year. Some cookies we decorate, some we leave plain. I use fresh root ginger in my recipe and I hope you will too—it really adds something special that powdered ginger lacks.

MAKES ABOUT 60

½ cup (115 g) butter
½ cup (100 g) granulated sugar
⅔ cup (110 g) molasses (treacle)
1 egg
1-inch (2.5-cm) piece of fresh root ginger, grated
    (use a fine grater like a micro-plane grater)
    or 1½ teaspoons ground ginger
1 teaspoon vanilla extract
1 teaspoon ground cinnamon
¼ teaspoon ground cloves
3 cups (400 g) all-purpose (plain) flour,
    plus extra for dusting
¾ teaspoon baking soda (bicarbonate of soda)

FOR THE BUTTER FROSTING:

½ cup (115 g) butter, at room temperature
3-4 cups (425-565 g) icing sugar
3-4 tablespoons light (single) cream or milk
1 teaspoon vanilla extract

1 Beat the butter and sugar together in a bowl until light and fluffy. Add the molasses, egg, fresh ginger, and vanilla extract.

2 Mix the spices, flour, and baking soda (bicarbonate of soda) together in a separate bowl.

3 Scrape the wet ingredients into the flour mixture and blend together well—you will have to use your hands as this is a dry dough. Gently knead the dough until it absorbs all the flour. Wrap up the dough in plastic wrap (clingfilm) and transfer to the fridge to chill for at least two hours, or overnight.

4 Preheat the oven to 350°F/180°C/Gas 4 and line a baking sheet with parchment (greaseproof) paper.

5 Unwrap the dough and roll it out on a lightly floured surface.

BROWN BUTTER FROSTING: Use the same ingredients for the frosting, but melt the butter in a small saucepan first and let it brown—not burn, just begin to brown. Remove it from the heat. Blend the brown butter with the icing sugar, cream, and vanilla the same as for the butter frosting. Browning the butter gives a really good flavor to the frosting.

Lightly flour a rolling pin so the dough doesn't stick and roll the dough out to about ¼ in (5 mm) thick. If you want crispy cookies, roll the dough thinner. If you want softer cookies, keep the dough thicker.

6 You can now use cookie cutters to cut out shapes of your choice. We like to use trees, moose, wolves, stars, squirrels ... a little less traditional, but fun. If you plan to hang them on a tree or tie them to a present, use a straw to poke a hole in the top of each cookie. Place them on the prepared baking sheet.

7 Bake your shapes in the preheated oven for 8–10 minutes until the edges are just slightly brown.

8 While the cookies are cooling make your frosting. Beat the butter in a bowl until smooth. Begin to add the icing sugar, 1 cup (140 g) at a time. After you have added 3 cups (425 g) of icing sugar, add 3 tablespoons of cream and the vanilla. You can either keep the frosting thick and spread it on with a knife, or add a bit more cream so you can use a piping bag to apply the frosting.

9 Once the cookies have cooled, you can decorate them as preferred. I like butter frosting and any chance I get to eat it, is a happy day.

MACAROONS

When I was a kid, my mom made a version of these cookies with sugar and oatmeal, which we loved. My sister and I would secretly make them when she was at work and split them. This is a new, healthy twist on that cookie—now I don't have to feel so bad when I eat half the batch.

MAKES 18

3 cups (210 g) organic shredded dried coconut (I like a finer grind)

½ cup (50 g) good-quality cocoa powder

¼ cup (40 g) coconut oil, at room temperature so it's mixable

6 tablespoons real maple syrup

1   Add all the ingredients to a bowl and mix well.

2   Use a spoon to scoop out some mixture and form into little little balls. Place them on a baking sheet lined with parchment (greaseproof) paper and let sit about an hour ... but let's be serious, I've never let them set before I started to eat them.

RICE PUDDING WITH CARDAMOM

I think this is the only other thing I remember my mom making. She baked hers in the oven and put raisins in, but I still ate it. To me, this could be breakfast, lunch, and dinner—especially good topped with pistachio nuts.

SERVES 4

1 cup (170–180 g) basmati rice
2 ½ cups (360 ml) low-fat or whole milk
one 14-oz (400-g) can coconut milk
1 teaspoon vanilla extract
½ cup (100 g) granulated sugar
5 cardamom pods, seeds removed and crushed to a fine
    powder with a mortar and pestle

1 Place all the ingredients in a large saucepan. Bring to a boil and then simmer for 20 minutes. Ready! It will be very creamy and delicious.

2 If for some odd reason you don't eat it all, keep it in the fridge. It will become very solid, but add a bit of milk or cream to loosen it up before eating. A few seconds in the microwave will help, too.

MINI JAM PIES

My daughter has no idea what a pop tart is—isn't that wonderful? I grew up on them—isn't that awful?

MAKES 3-4 MINI PIES

1 batch of pastry (see page 48)—add 1 tablespoon granulated
    sugar to the dough when making this recipe
Light (single) cream and granulated sugar, for sprinkling

FOR THE FILLING:

Anything goes really. You will need about 2-3 tablespoons of filling for
    each mini pie—you can use some of your apple sauce (see page 128),
    any flavor of jam, or even nutella
Flour, for thickening (this is only needed if you are using jam or
    any other slightly runny filling)

TIP: You can make any shape you like for these—hearts are always loved. If you don't have much time but want to make a treat for the family, thaw out some puff pastry, roll it out, fill with jam, fold over and bake for 15 minutes at 400 °F / 200 °C / Gas 6.

1 Preheat the oven to 350°F/180°C/Gas 4.

2 Roll out your prepared dough (make sure you have added the sugar) on a lightly floured work surface. Cut out 6–8 rectangles about 3½ x 5 in (8 x 12.5 cm) depending on the size you want your mini pies to be. (I made six and had some extra dough for another day.)

3 Place one rectangle of pastry on a baking sheet lined with parchment (greaseproof) paper.

4 Put 3 tablespoons of your filling (we used Missing Goat Raspberry Jam) in a bowl (add a teaspoon of flour if it is slightly runny and looks like it needs thickening up a bit.) Mix well.

5 Spoon the mixture into the center of each pastry rectangle. Lay your next rectangle on top and use a fork to seal the edges. Repeat with your other pastry pieces to make 3–4 mini pies.

6 Brush some cream on top of each pie with a pastry brush. Sprinkle with sugar or some cinnamon.

7 Bake the mini pies in the preheated oven for 20 minutes. Then you could drizzle on some frosting (see page 144) or just enjoy them as they are.

FRUIT AND SEED CRACKERS

I love crackers. I love that this recipe makes so many crackers, and that you can store them away in the freezer until needed. We make these all year round, but they would be a great holiday party cracker, or the perfect gift for a friend. They are delicious with raisins and walnuts. I put goat's cheese and rhubarb jam (see page 29) on mine. You will need to get your hands on some mini loaf pans. My mom had a silicone set of four, so I stole them.

MAKES 80-90

2 cups (275 g) wholewheat flour
2 teaspoons baking soda (bicarbonate of soda)
¼ cup (50 g) brown sugar
2 teaspoons salt
2 tablespoons apple cider vinegar
2 cups (460 ml) low-fat or whole milk
⅓ cup (90 g) runny honey
1 cup (140 g) raisins or dried apricots
½ cup (65 g) whole almonds
½ cup (65 g) pistachio nuts
½ cup (70 g) sunflower seeds
¼ cup (30 g) hemp heart seeds
¼ cup (20 g) Gruyére cheese, grated

1 Mix the flour, baking soda (bicarbonate of soda), brown sugar, and salt together in a bowl. Mix the apple cider vinegar and milk together in a jug or bowl and then pour this into the flour mix. Mix all together well. Add the honey and stir together. Add the remaining ingredients and mix well.

2 Pour the mixture into four non-stick mini loaf pans and bake them in the preheated oven for about 35–40 minutes until firm and cooked through. Remove from the oven and let cool.

3 Now, put them in the freezer. What? Why? I'll tell you. You need them to firm up so you can slice them really thin. Freezing them for four hours (says my neighbor Judy) is the perfect time—not frozen solid, as I tried to do. (If you do freeze them overnight, just let them sit for about 10 minutes before you begin to slice them.) The key is to cut them thinly to get the ultimate crispy cracker.

4 Once cut, lay them on a baking sheet. Bake in an oven preheated to 350°F/180°C/Gas 4 for 8 minutes. Remove from the oven, flip, and then bake for another 8 minutes. Let cool and enjoy.

TIP: If you put these in a bag or container, they will go soft. I leave mine out on the counter and they stay crisp. But if they do go soft, just put them in the oven for a few minutes and they will crisp right up for you.

NOTE: I add preserved lemons to almost everything—hummus, roast chicken, any kind of fish, granola bars, scrambled eggs, quiche, or tarts—they're crazy good and so simple.

PRESERVED MEYER LEMONS

My friend Noelle brought me the most beautiful Meyer lemons from her home in Palm Springs. I made preserved lemons. I had to see what all the fuss was about. Anyone who has used them, swears they are spectacular—AND IT'S TRUE. I hope you try them. Oh, and zest the lemons you squeeze for juice and then see below for some ways to use the zest.

MAKES 1 X 24-FL OZ (750-ML) JAR

8-10 Meyer lemons
⅔ cup (130 g) medium coarse salt
Olive oil

1 Cut off the pointy bottoms and stem tops of 6 lemons (save the rest for juicing) and slice each lemon into 8 wedges. Cut out the center pith and remove the seeds. Throw them in a bowl with the salt. Toss them around until they are all coated. Scoop them into a 17 fl oz (500 ml) canning jar.

2 Juice the remaining lemons and pour the juice into the jar—you want to cover the lemons in the jar completely in the juice.

3 Leave the jar on your counter, out of direct sunlight, on a tea towel or plate. Why? Because I didn't and some of the juice leaked out and ate away a circle in my counter ... oops.

4 Each day, once or twice, turn them upside down and give them a shake. Do this for five days.

5 Then add ¼ cup (60 ml) of olive oil and refrigerate. The lemons are ready to be used after another five days and will keep in the fridge for 6-8 months.

6 When you want to use some lemons, remove however many wedges you need and give them a good rinse under the tap. The salt is really, really strong, and it goes right through the lemon. Chop up the lemon extra fine, or mash with the side of a knife.

7 Add to any dish that calls for some lemon and mix through well. You will need to experiment as the flavor is very strong. You may like more or less, but it depends on the dish.

Using lemon zest

• If you have lemons filling your kitchen like I always seem to have, you begin to think about other ways to use them. I had Meyer lemons up the yahoo and we zested half of them for lemon curd, but needed just a few tablespoons. So, I dried some, sprinkled on a piece of parchment (greaseproof) paper on a baking sheet for two days. Once it's dry, you can mix it in with a really good-quality salt—perfect for cooking with.
• You can also freeze lemon zest to use when needed. Freeze it on the baking sheet first, before putting it in a bag, so it doesn't freeze in clumps.
• You can also put some dried zest in sugar ... lemon sugar! Perfect for cookies, cakes, and pies. Also, what a pretty gift to give someone.

BLUEBERRY SYRUP

I'm a big fan of real maple syrup, but a warm blueberry syrup on crêpes will put a big smile on my face any day. This also makes a nice gift.

MAKES ABOUT 3 CUPS (500 ML)

4 cups (500 g) blueberries (fresh or frozen)
1 cup (240 ml) water
¾ cup (150 g) granulated sugar
¼ teaspoon ground cinnamon
A wedge of Preserved Lemon (see page 153), rinsed well
   and finely chopped, or some lemon zest (optional)

1 Put all the ingredients in a saucepan. Bring to a boil and stir until the sugar has dissolved. Simmer over low to medium heat for 10 minutes. Remove from the heat and let cool.

2 If you like lumpy blueberries in a sauce, you are done. If you like a smooth sauce, either run this through a fine sieve on the food mill, or press through a strainer (sieve) with a spoon.

3 Decant into sterilized jars or an airtight container. This can be kept in the fridge for weeks and used on French Toast or Bread Pudding (see page 135), ice cream, pancakes ...

DOG BISCUITS

Ollie came into our lives at Christmas and he hasn't stopped eating since. He cleans out our strawberry patch, broccoli bed, tomatoes, and post-it notes, and even ate the trunk of the cherry tree ... Why do we need to make him treats, too? Because, look at that face.

MAKES ... LOTS
(ABOUT 100 IF CUT INTO SQUARES)

1 cup (140 g) oats
2½ cups (340 g) wholewheat flour, plus extra for dusting
⅓ cup (75 g) peanut butter
⅛ cup (10 g) wheatgerm
⅛ cup (15 g) ground flax seeds
⅛ cup (15 g) oat bran
¼ cup (35 g) sunflower seeds
3 tablespoons olive oil
1½ cups (360 ml) hot water
A handful of parsley, freshly chopped

1 Preheat the oven to 325°F/160°C/Gas 3.

2 Mix together all the ingredients in a large bowl. Start off using a spoon as the mixture is hot, but then switch to your hands as the mixture cools.

3 Use some extra wholewheat flour to dust the work surface and then roll out the dough. It's a big batch, so you may need to do half a batch at a time.

4 We use the pizza cutter to cut into squares—it's super-fast—but Lily always likes to make hearts or squirrel shapes for Oliver, too.

5 Bake in the preheated oven for 25–30 minutes. Check them after 20 minutes if you have cut them small—they should be just lightly browned and feel dry. I over-cooked them once, but Ollie really didn't mind.

GARLIC MASH FOR CHICKENS

Yes, I have spoilt chickens. But I figure they are giving us beautiful rich eggs, and the better they eat, the better we eat. Our egg yolks are the most stunning orange I've ever seen. I only have five chickens, so it's easy to spoil a small flock, and what better time to do this than in the cold wet winter. We give them this mash on really dreadful days, along with individual little yogurt sundaes, organic feeds, and a melon or two.

This mash is served warm and every speck of it is soon gone. You can add or omit any of the flax or chia seeds—we really use whatever we have on hand—but the garlic is really good for chickens; it's an old-fashioned way of fighting off bugs and worms in, or on, your birds.

**MAKES ENOUGH TO FEED
5 SOGGY CHICKENS**

2 cups (280 g) oats
2 cups (480 ml) boiling water
1 banana, chopped
⅛ cup (10 g) chia seed
⅛ cup (15 g) ground flax seed
⅛ cup (15 g) oat bran
⅛ cup (10 g) wheatgerm
2 tablespoons olive oil
2–3 garlic cloves, crushed
A handful of raisins

1 Put the oats and hot water in a large bowl and give it a good stir. Throw in everything else, except the raisins. Mix well and just let cool to the point that you can touch it and it feels warm. We don't want burnt beaks!

2 I have a very old muffin pan that I have designated as the mash pan. I divide the mash into the muffin holes and then sprinkle the raisins on top. It's ready to go—no baking involved. Serve to your gals and they will love you all the more.

INDEX

Picture Credits

Heather Cameron © pp. 11, 13 top, 17, 24, 46, 82, 83, 86, 109 bottom left, 110 top right
Kim Christie © pp. 3, 13 bottom, 14, 15, 34, 55 centre left, 117, 118, 119, 144
Janis Nicolay © jacket back flap, pp. 5, 6, 19 bottom, 48, 49
All other images are by Heather Cameron and © CICO Books.

Acknowledgments

Thanks to Noelle Rawlins for the Meyer Lemon Curd label on page 44 and the yellow boots on page 133.